GLOBAL POLITICAL STUDIES

VICTIMS AND EXECUTIONERS

AMERICAN POLITICAL DISCOURSES ON THE HOLOCAUST FROM LIBERATION TO BITBURG

GLOBAL POLITICAL STUDIES

Additional books in this series can be found on Nova's website under the Series tab.

Additional e-books in this series can be found on Nova's website under the e-book tab.

GLOBAL POLITICAL STUDIES

VICTIMS AND EXECUTIONERS

AMERICAN POLITICAL DISCOURSES ON THE HOLOCAUST FROM LIBERATION TO BITBURG

BINOY KAMPMARK

NOVINKA

New York

For permission to use material from this book please contact us:
Telephone 631-231-7269; Fax 631-231-8175
Web Site: http://www.novapublishers.com

NOTICE TO THE READER

LIBRARY OF CONGRESS CATALOGING-IN-PUBLICATION DATA

ISBN: 978-1-62417-861-0

Published by Nova Science Publishers, Inc. † New York

CONTENTS

Preface		**vii**
Acknowledgment		
Chapter 1	Introduction: Victims and Executioners	**1**
Chapter 2	The Politics of the Executioner	**27**
Chapter 3	The Eichmann Trial	**59**
Chapter 4	Reconciliation at Bitburg	**83**
Chapter 5	Reflections	**105**
Index		**113**

Preface

In recent years, much has been written on how the moral meaning and significance of the Holocaust has been appropriated in popular and political discourses in the United States. Authors such as Peter Novick and Norman Finkelstein have argued that the Holocaust has been "Americanized," often detracting from its European origins and the problematic moral questions it poses. This work goes further by focusing on the particular framing of the Holocaust in U.S. official and public discourses with particular reference to foreign policy debate and how this contrasts with the "civil religion" of Holocaust commemoration in the United States. It traces the way in which such debates have been structured around various assumptions made about the victims on the one hand, and executioners on the other. It also traces how the relationship between the Jewish victims and German executioners in American public discourse has been affected by pragmatic and political considerations at various historical junctures, particularly those concerning the Federal Republic of Germany and the State of Israel.

ACKNOWLEDGMENTS

This work formed the basis of a thesis in Master of Philosophy in history completed at the University of Queensland under the direction of Dr. Andrew Bonnell. His razor sharp awareness and sensitivity to the issues, which surfaced during this work were a revelation. I have various others to thank – those who combed through my writing, offering extremely useful insights. Joseph Siracusa and Dirk Moses offered invaluable suggestions. Mistakes that arise in this text are mine and mine alone. I also give personal thanks to the various staff at the Library of Congress in Washington, D.C. and the National Archives in Maryland who provided excellent facilities in researching and writing this work. St. John's College within the University of Queensland, and its Warden, Professor John Morgan, provided the convivial surroundings that enabled me to write this piece. Personal thanks are extended to innumerable colleagues and friends during that time who made my stay at the University enjoyable. They know who they are.

Binoy Kampmark
Melbourne, 2012

Chapter 1

INTRODUCTION: VICTIMS AND EXECUTIONERS

When you enter the United States on the non-visa waiver programme, one question becomes noticeable on consulting the application form. It stands out in contrast to other sections, officious, demanding attention: "Have you ever been or are you now involved in espionage; or in terrorist activities; or genocide; or between 1933 and 1945 were you involved, in any way, in persecutions associated with Nazi Germany or its allies?"[1] When you enter the United States Holocaust Museum, civilization's realisation of its own tragic potential is impressed upon the visitor.[2] You are given a card. You are acquainted with a victim displayed on the card, engaging a narrative that leads to an unfolding story of genocide. Both instances reveal a particular legacy: the influence of the Holocaust in distinct spaces of American collective memory. So significant has this development been that the U.S. Holocaust Museum has perhaps gone one step further than Yad Vashem in communicating a sense of the event.

At first glance there is a consistency in their themes. They express the same voice. Both domestically and internationally, the Holocaust and genocide are manifestations of an evil that American society repudiates and punishes. The United States is idealised as the key "defender" of minority rights globally, a proponent of humanitarian intervention. Under the Obama administration, an Atrocities Prevention Board has been created for developing

---

[1] U.S. Department of Justice, I-94 W Nonimmigrant Visa Waiver Arrival/Departure Form, Immigration and Naturalization Service, OMB No. 1115-0148, copy in author's possession.

[2] This characterisation of the Holocaust is from Zygmunt Bauman, *Modernity and the Holocaust* (Ithaca: Cornell University Press, 2000).

strategies in prioritising US policies in preventing the occurrence of grave human rights abuses.[3] "The Atrocities Prevention Board is the administration's organizational hub for tracking international threats and using intelligence, diplomacy and other tools to defuse them."[4]

But when one analyses the voice of Holocaust public and official discourse for uniform patterns of moral outrage, differences emerge. Elie Wiesel, who was appointed by President Jimmy Carter in 1978 to the Commission on the Holocaust argues that Holocaust memories should never be political.[5] Those entrusted as caretakers and interpreters of such memories must, instead, embrace an ethical mission. This has hardly been the case, notably in policies privileging the welfare of executioners at the expense of the victims. The Cold War context is particularly striking in this regard. The German agents responsible for perpetrating the killings became redeemable. At the very least, they could be accommodated in post-Nazi Germany in the name of broader national interests. This approach in American political debates, particular in its foreign policy, was one of tactics and Realpolitik. Such an interpretation is not marketed in the United States Holocaust Museum, which carefully avoids the various contradictions of American debates on such matters as war crimes politics. The museum is grim but redolent with an image of "Zionist closure", where, as Omer Bartov argues, optimistic America mobilizes the representation of the Final Solution in a manner that "asserts humanity's march toward a better future, all accidents and misfortunes notwithstanding."[6]

The museum's aspiration is a footnote in the American hope that promotes a different view of the Final Solution, one out of step with American political and legal discourses that focused on forced reconciliation, forgiveness, and the equitable treatment of war criminals in the early years of the Cold War. Such an account is conspicuously absent. The moral representation of the Holocaust in the Museum, for that reason, masks the historical conflict within American political discourses to how best to deal with the implications of that event.

---

[3] Human Rights First, "President Obama Announces Creation of Atrocities Prevention Board," Press Release, April 23, 2012.

[4] Eric Roston, "The Atrocities Prevention Board Badly Needs a New Name," *Bloomberg Businessweek*, April 24, 2012.

[5] Mark Chmiel, "The Political Varieties of Sacred Remembrance: Elie Wiesel and U.S. Foreign Policy," *Journal of Church and State* 40, 4 (Autumn, 1998): 827.

[6] Omer Bartov, *Murder in Our Midst: The Holocaust, Industrial Killing and Representation* (New York: Oxford University Press, 1996), 9.

AMERICANIZATION

If we are to understand the Holocaust in the context of how American political discourses have interrogated its significance, it is insufficient to merely document it at the level of how American public groups have appropriated it as their own moral lodestone. On this level, there is a growing historiography, much of it accepting the notion that the Holocaust has been "Americanized".[7] Unlike other distant calamities such as the Armenian atrocities and the Balkan atrocities of the 1990s, the Holocaust in time overcame geographical and emotional distance to be entrenched within American collective consciousness in what David Chidester and Edward T. Linenthal have called "American sacred space."[8] Others have deemed it an "ethnic adjunct to American civil religion".[9] In time, it was distinguished from the Nuremberg trials to occupy a central position in American consciousness, displacing rival atrocities and crimes in terms of importance.[10] This came in the wake of numerous works which have their own potential in rendering the Holocaust relevant in American life, namely those studies which have emphasised "closed doors" and western indifference to Jewish refugees.[11] Walter Laqueur's pioneering study on the "closed door" after the start of World War II, noting the refusal of Western nations, most notably the United States, to take further action on the massacres against Jews, paved the way for detailed studies that have shown the ambivalent attitudes of the Allies in

---

[7] Hilene Flanzbaum, ed., *The Americanization of the Holocaust* (Baltimore: John Hopkins University Press, 1999); Michael Berenbaum, "The Nativization of the Holocaust," in *After Tragedy and Triumph: Modern Jewish Thought and the American Experience* (Cambridge: Cambridge University Press, 1990), 3-16.

[8] David Chidester and Edward T. Linenthal, *American Sacred Space* (Bloomington, IN: Indiana University Press, 1995). The study of how effective this entrenchment has been can be gathered in James E. Young, *The Texture of Memory: Holocaust Memorials and Meaning* (New Haven: Yale University Press, 1993).

[9] Chmiel, "The Political Varieties of Sacred Remembrance," 827.

[10] To see how the Holocaust became particular after the more general narrative of German atrocities at Nuremberg, see Robert K. Woetzel, *The Nuremberg Trials in International Law with a Postlude on the Eichmann Case* (New York: Frederick A. Praeger, Inc., 1962).

[11] Richard Breitman and Alan M. Kraut, *American Refugee policy and European Jewry, 1933-1945* (Bloomington: Indiana University Press, 1987); David S. Wyman, *The Abandonment of the Jews: America and the Holocaust, 1941-1945* (New York: Pantheon Books, 1984); *Paper Walls: America and the Refugee Crisis, 1938-1941* (New York: Pantheon Books, 1985). More recently, see Richard Breitman, *Official Secrets: What the Nazis Planned, What the British and Americans Knew* (London: Penguin, 2000). For a contrary position on how the European Jewry could not have been saved, see William D. Rubenstein, *The Myth of Closed Doors: Why the Democracies Could Not Have Saved More Jews From the Nazis* (London: Routledge, 1997).

attempting to prevent atrocities or any substantive rescue of European Jewry from extermination.[12] This particular field of Holocaust literature is considerable, heavily covered in histories that take sides on the issue of Western attitudes to Jewish immigration. They are lamentations of failed prevention, forming the vanguard of narratives on the earlier part of the Third Reich, when Jews, instead of featuring as the victims of crematoria and camps, should have been welcomed as refugees escaping persecution by various countries'.

The Holocaust has preoccupied scholars from numerous angles, and the Americanization of it is but one aspect of this. There are enduring arguments about intentionalism and functionalism, the paper trail to the murderers as they pondered the Final Solution, the functioning of the camps and the moral impoverishment they signified for civilization as a whole.[13] There is a growing comparative literature on how the Holocaust has featured in discourses on genocidal events in Bosnia, Rwanda and Kosovo.[14] There are debates on the appropriateness of comparing the Holocaust to such events and attempts to "Judaeize" them. René Lemarchand has argued that drawing out similar threads between the Holocaust and the Rwandan genocide is a lazy exercise that skirts over different historical contexts: the Tutsis, unlike the Jews, he observes, were a threat to the internal order of the state.[15] A German study has engaged the manipulation of Holocaust tropes in the Kosovo war, arguing that the culture of memory in the 1990s has been significantly shaped by the legacy

[12] Walter Laqueur, *The Terrible Secret: An Investigation into the Suppression of Information About Hitler's 'Final Solution'* (London: Weidenfeld & Nicholson, 1980).

[13] The intentionalist and functionalist aspect on the origins of the Holocaust was coined in 1981 by Timothy Mason, "Intention and Explanation: A Current Controversy about the Interpretation of National Socialism" in *Der Führerstaat, Mythos und Realität: Studien zur Struktur und Politik des Dritten Reiches* or The Fuhrer State: Myth and Reality: studies on the structure and politics of the Third Reich (Stuttgart: Klett-Cotta, 1981). For the impact of Auschwitz, some titles are appropriate: Martin Gilbert, *Auschwitz and the Allies* (London: Michael Joseph, 1981) in the field of diplomacy and tactics; Terrence Des Pres, *The Survivor: An Anatomy of Life in the Death Camps* (New York: Pocket Books, 1977) on the psychology of survival; Yisrael Gutman and Michael Berenbaum, eds., *Anatomy of the Auschwitz Death Camp* (Bloomington, Ind: Indiana University Press and the United States Holocaust Memorial Museum, 1994).

[14] For Bosnia and Kosovo, see Marla Stone, "When Memory Shapes Policy: Bosnia, Kosovo, and the Holocaust," *New England Journal of History* 59 (2-3) (2002-3): 18-41.

[15] René Lemarchand, "Disconnecting the Threads: Rwanda and the Holocaust Reconsidered," *Journal of Genocide Research* 4, 4 (2002): 499-518. See also William F. S. Miles, "Hamites and Hebrews: Problems in 'Judaizing' the Rwandan Genocide," *Journal of Genocide Research* 2, 1 (2000): 107-115; Catherine Newbury and David Newbury, "The Genocide in Rwanda and the Holocaust in Germany: Parallels and Pitfalls," *Journal of Genocide Research* 5, 1 (2003): 135-145.

of Auschwitz.[16] Such Holocaust literature has generated its own commemorative effect, debating and renewing the boundaries of its legacies. So pervasive has the discussion of the event proven that scholars have decided that it merits encyclopaedias, voluminous accounts and bibliographies.[17] Much primary source documentation has also made it into the public sphere.[18] In light of all this, the fears on the part of academics that the Holocaust might be fading are unfounded.[19]

The idea of an Americanized Holocaust is one that has much empirical evidence to support it. American newspapers regularly report ceremonies honouring Holocaust survivors.[20] Education programs in the United States incorporating pedagogical techniques commemorating the Holocaust are frequent. In July 2000, FBI Director Louis J. Freeh went so far as to announce that his agency had begun a new program of education for new recruits on the Holocaust to emphasise "the horror and evil which can result from not just a government, but particularly law enforcement, abandoning its mission to protect people and becoming the engine of oppression."[21]

At a cultural level, the influence has also been felt, with a *sui generis* European event, interpreted as a moral archetype that conditions behaviour in the pattern of absolute good and absolute evil. Its historical participants regarded as either innocent victims or irredeemable murderers. The Americanized Holocaust has also resulted in fierce political struggles over its legacy, conflicts which reveal "serious divisions" within its various discourses.[22]

---

[16] Jacob Günther, "Die Metaphern Des Holocaust Während Des Kosovokriegs," *1999: Zeitschrift für Sozialgeschichte des 20. und 21. Jahrhunderts* 15, 1 (2000): 160-183.

[17] Some examples are: Israel Gutman, ed., *Encyclopaedia of the Holocaust* (New York: Macmillan, 1990), 4 volumes; Donald Niewyk and Francis Nicosia, eds., *The Columbia Guide to the Holocaust* (New York: Columbia University Press, 2000); John K. Roth and Elisabeth Maxwell, eds., *Remembering for the Future: The Holocaust in an Age of Genocide* (New York: Palgrave, 2001), 3 volumes; David S. Wyman, ed., *The World Reacts to the Holocaust* (Baltimore: John Hopkins University Press, 1996).

[18] See for instance, Raul Hilberg, ed., *Documents of Destruction: Germany and Jewry, 1933-1945* (Chicago: Quadrangle Books, 1971), and the large collection in John Mendelsohn, *The Holocaust: Selected Documents in 18 Volumes* (New York: Garland, 1982).

[19] For such fears, see Deborah E. Lipstadt, *Denying the Holocaust: The Growing Assault on Truth and Memory* (New York: Free Press, 1993); and the formidable work by Pierre Vidal-Naquet, *Assassins of Memory: Essays on the Denial of the Holocaust,* trans. Jeffrey Mehlman (New York: Columbia University Press, 1992).

[20] For example, see the *Post-Standard* (Syracuse, NY), "Oswego State to Honor Refugee From Holocaust," September 11, 2002, B1.

[21] Quoted in the *Arkansas Democrat-Gazette*, July 1, 2000, A1.

[22] John K. Roth, "How is the Holocaust Best Remembered? Reflections on History, Religion and Morality after the Holocaust," in Roth et al, *Remembering for the Future*, 394-409, 394.

We find a notable example of this Holocaust archetype in the art exhibit "Mirroring Evil: Nazi Imagery/Recent Art" by the Jewish Museum in New York in 2002, where the Americanized Holocaust came to the fore as a peerless, inalienable moral standard. Steven C. Munson, described as "an artist and civil servant" living in Washington D.C., chose to distinguish a previous provocative exhibit at the Brooklyn Exhibit of Art named "Sensation" (1999) with "Mirroring Evil." While "Sensation" was an affront to Roman Catholics, they were not Jews "who have a definite interest in how the 'issue' of the Holocaust is treated". The mistake made by the Jewish Museum was its pedagogical approach in taking "its organizing theme [as] a historical event of considerable significance" then seeking to instruct "us in its 'lessons' for today." But when it came to the specifics of the Holocaust as history, Munson did not find these "lessons" palatable in light of debates after the terrorist attacks on the U.S. on September 11, 2001. No art could make its targets the "current lotuses of veil in the world" as "America and Israel": Israel could not be condemned, as the artist Alan Schechner had suggested, through its use of the Holocaust to justify "unsavoury" policies in times of "self-defence"; the United States should have been immune from any "morally undermining critique of American consumer culture".[23]

These trends towards the Americanization of the Holocaust underscore a significant point, namely, the political subtleties of how it was viewed in various theatres outside the United States.

How American political discourses on the Holocaust deal with framing the dialectic between the politics of the victim and executioner remains a relatively unexplored area of the literature, especially in debates within the United States on how to respond to German war crimes and Israel's capture of Eichmann. Here a distinction has to be made between the discursive practice on the Holocaust, with its moral triangulations, qualifications, and interventions, and the moral starkness of the Holocaust itself.

The spectacle of thousands of humans being carted to the gas chambers is devoid of dialectical and theoretical reduction. Rather, it is the interpretative framework around the Holocaust, the debates in American political circles about the Final Solution as it unfolded outside the U.S. that form the subject of this inquiry.

What role did the Final Solution play in policy debates on how to rehabilitate Germany for its Cold War struggles? What was the position taken by American observers of the Eichmann trial in Jerusalem? In both cases, the

[23] Steven C. Munson, "Nazis, Jews, and 'Mirroring Evil'," *Commentary* 113, 5 (May 2002): 60-4.

attitudes prove somewhat contradictory, most notably on the level of how the respective victims and executioners of the Holocaust were treated.

This position contrasts with the current assumption in American readings of the Holocaust which have accepted its moral value as irreducible, where one is directed to "identify with the victims." Peter Novick notes why this might be so – moral clarity in an otherwise morally obtuse world, providing Americans divided by ideology, generations and ethics with "a moral reference point" of unity.[24] But this interpretive framework of the Holocaust should not be taken to suppose that its legacy has not been manipulated. Novick's work does more than realise the subtle plays on Holocaust memory that have taken place in the forming of American collective consciousness. The Holocaust as a metaphor was used to "support anti-Communist interventions abroad", by participants in anti-abortion debates, and to warn the American public against moral indifference.[25] In the United States, the emblematic survivor of human cruelty has been used as an influential model of invoking discussion on the Holocaust. But as Novick has made clear, the Holocaust as historical reality, being singular and inimitable, is not as useful a pedagogical motif as advocates of its legacy suggest.[26]

Far from focusing exclusively on the emblematic survivor or heroic victim, American political discourses on the Final Solution, whether in its juridical or political sense, reveal deep contradictions, exposing a dichotomy between how the victim and executioner have been represented and discussed. The attitudes towards executioners and victims have proven fluid, whether in the easing of the new Federal Germany into the security framework of Europe in the 1950s where war criminals featured as bargaining chips, or the responses to the Eichmann trial, where the roles of victim and executioner are juggled by conservative and extreme groups more concerned with communism than seeing the Jews as *sui generis* victims of Nazi terror. Ultimately, this political dichotomy is realized as a misguided catharsis at the Bitburg ceremonies of 1985 which commemorated a different sort of German to the camp guards of the 1940s.

To this end, the investigation, once taken further, examines how this co-opting of the Holocaust in American official and political debate conceals the working of tensions around the ethical and juridical conflicts between the executioner and the victim. The modern discourse on the Holocaust might restore such moral notions as radical evil – the recent work on Eichmann does

---

[24] Peter Novick, *The Holocaust and Collective Memory* (London: Bloomsbury, 2000), 13.
[25] Novick, *Holocaust and Collective Memory*, 12.
[26] Novick, *Holocaust and Collective Memory*, 12-15.

much to suggest it, notwithstanding the arguments put forth by Hannah Arendt which categorise his crimes as the product of bureaucratic banality.[27] But the subtleties of the discourse have been hidden in an overall critique of how the Holocaust has been used, or "vulgarised".[28] Boaz Evron's critique of Israel's use of the Holocaust provides an example. He argues that Israel's reliance on the Holocaust credo forced West Germany "to act against its natural interest [...] and accord Israel a special preference, without Israel feeling obliged to pay Germany back with the hard currency of reciprocal interests".[29] Israel, and its citizens, were inserted into an ahistorical continuum, insisting on being treated as "abnormal", "a sect divorced from historical process."[30] Evron's critique must be evaluated in the context of historical fact and discursive exploitation. Some literature points to the exploitation of the Holocaust in the name of the victim as faulty, allowing avenues of politicisation along the lines of identity.[31] But such work is clearly not intended to challenge the authenticity of the victim's plight or the executioner's responsibility, but more to critique the representation of their legacy in other contexts. In Evron's case, the use was geopolitical, thereby undermining the sacral essence of the victim's suffering.

The legacy of this critique of the Holocaust has been continued in such works as those of Peter Novick and Norman G. Finkelstein.[32] These authors critique the cultural and political use of the Holocaust as a distinct American phenomenon, though the slant both authors take does not question the moral quality of the Holocaust narrative, nor the moral-ethical position of the victims as such. Finkelstein argues that the Holocaust "industry" sprung from a social conscience that constructed and aggrandized the relevance of the event, with

---

[27] For the argument of Eichmann as a representative of radical evil, see Alessandro Ferrara, "A Meditation on Radical Evil from a Postmetaphysical Point of View," in María Pía Lara, ed., *Rethinking Evil: Contemporary Perspectives* (Berkeley: University of California, 2001), 173-188, 183.

[28] Michael Marrus, *The Holocaust in History* (Hanover: University Press of New England, 1987), 202.

[29] Boaz Evron, "Holocaust: The Uses of Disaster," *Radical America* 17, 4 (July-August 1983): 7-21, 13.

[30] Evron, "Holocaust," 14; and see Roth, "How is the Holocaust Best Remembered?," 394. For the American angle that the Holocaust was being abused in the Eichmann trial to damage US-West German interests, see examples in Novick, *Holocaust and Collective Memory*, 129-30; "Thoughts on Eichmann," *National Review* 10 (April 22, 1961): 238-9; "Let's All Hate Germany, Comrade," *National Review* 10 (March 25, 1961): 172.

[31] See Jean-Michel Chaumont, *La concurrence des victims: Génocide, identité, reconnaissance* (Paris: Editions La Découverte, 1997), 137.

[32] Novick, *The Holocaust and Collective Memory*; Norman G. Finkelstein, *The Holocaust Industry: Reflections on the Exploitation of Jewish Suffering* (London: Verso, 2000).

ideologues cognitively geared to idealise the language of Holocaust commemoration. "The abnormality [of discourses] of the Nazi holocaust springs not from the event itself but from the exploitive industry that has grown up around it." This is an "ideological representation of the Nazi holocaust" which as a consequence, "bears a connection, if tenuous, with reality".[33] Finkelstein is not seeking to problematize the ethics of the victim-executioner, rather, his inquiry is one based on an industry that ignores the moral issues of the Holocaust as history, where its memory becomes the means to an end, whether through financial compensation or the excoriation of critics of Israel.

Works such as Novick's and Finkelstein's commence an inquiry into Holocaust discourse as a credo that requires examination, but do not pursue the more complex issues of how American political debates distinguish the positioning of the victim and executioner in the debates. To comprehend the dominance of the Holocaust credo in American consciousness is not accurately explained by the assertion that it has become a moral lodestone, as Novick contends. Both works tend to critique the gradual Americanization of the Holocaust, ignoring the fundamental distinctions on how German atrocities were evaluated by Americans in the diachronic context, and how the fallen German executioner in political discourses became the heroic (or misunderstood, wounded) German in subsequent interpretations of the Cold War. Earlier debates on the Holocaust in the United States and by American officials in Germany reveal a focus on perpetrators, not victims, a view that has not been drawn out in Novick's and Finkelstein's work. The memory of the Holocaust was not sacrosanct from the viewpoint of those who suffered it, since the authorities in question, namely, the United States forces in occupation, were less interested in realising a victim-ideal than a strategic reordering of German-U.S. relations. Its realisation as a historical record was only dependent on how American officials recorded it: from this angle, it remains a record of diminished sentences, and political considerations.

There are also issues with Novick's use of evidence. A survey of his work does not focus in depth, for instance, on the direct commentary of American political leaders on the specific use of the Holocaust in American social life, let alone its foreign policy. There are some references scattered through the work, but the focus is mainly, as one reviewer rightly points out, "community groups" centred around "the internal memoranda of the American Jewish Committee or to articles in the *St. Petersburg Times*." The methodological approach in Novick focuses heavily on the use of synecdoche, where the small

[33] Finkelstein, *The Holocaust Industry*, 37.

becomes the whole; thus, a study of community reactions can be misread as a total explanation of Holocaust consciousness, underscoring more subtle conflicts such as the play-offs between debates on the victim and the perpetrator. The nature of these sources may not "actually *explain* why the Holocaust became central to American and political life".[34] While Novick leaves this aspect of the problem unanswered, it can at least be said that the Holocaust was treated with some ambiguity in political strategies adopted towards Germany as a post-war ally of the U.S. and Israel as the representative for global Jewry, which may go some way to explaining why it was not significant in earlier debates.

The paradigm of victim and executioner, and the politicisation of their respective roles is one of the significant features of these American debates on the Final Solution. These contours are peculiar in the space of U.S. foreign policy discourse and its interrogators – those numerous organizations of patriotic inclination and civic obligation who find reason to either suspect the use of Jewish victimhood, or in some cases, express revulsion at Washington's policy towards Germany as being too lenient. Such foreign policy discourse has depended more on Realpolitik than idealisations, despite the rhetoric to the contrary.

This strategy would seem to be inconsistent with the rhetoric that currently governs American political attitudes to the Holocaust in its global application. Wyman cites the chiselled words of three Presidents on the limestone of the U.S. Holocaust Museum in Washington: Jimmy Carter's "never again will the world stand silent" (September 1979); Ronald Reagan's announcement that humankind had to stare "this evil in the face" (October 1988); and George Bush's interventionist message: "Here we will learn that we must intervene when we see evil arise" (February 1991).[35] These evocations suggest a victim narrative, or at least the restoring of the victim to a pre-eminent position in modern political discourses of the Holocaust. This restoration would itself be implied by the existence of critiques against the triumph of victim politics. It is therefore timely to extend the discussion on the issue of how the Holocaust has been manipulated within the paradigm of victim-executioner politics. The literature at the moment is intractable in framing the Holocaust as either a unique unquestionable event in its universal relevance or the more subtle suggestion that its legacy has been misused or misunderstood in contemporary politics. A diachronic study of American

[34] Dan Stone, Review of Peter Novick, The Holocaust in American Life, in *European Journal of Social Theory* 5, 1 (January 2002): 165-8, 166.

[35] Wyman, "The United States," in Wyman, ed., *The World Reacts to the Holocaust*, 739.

debates on how the Holocaust was structured enables one to then view various strategies of Holocaust evocation and understanding within the framework of U.S. foreign policy and state interests. The welfare of victims (the Holocaust witness or victim of crimes against humanity) and the executioners (the SS, the Einsatzgruppen) is apposite in this regard.

Positioning the Victim and Executioner

Charting the typologies on how the politics of the victim and executioner conflict are reconciled (if at all) in American debates on the Holocaust is a useful method in surveying the debate on the alliance with Germany and Israel's trial of Eichmann.

The identity of the victim, destroyed by the totalitarian machinery of the Third Reich, would presumably have been restored, if not revered in heroic narratives and monuments of remembrance.[36] In other words, the discussions about punishing the perpetrators would surely have led to a more comprehensive empathising with the victims, most notably in Washington's approaches to its alliance with Germany.

It is hence useful to note the importance of what is meant by the "victim" in such debates. We would assume, given the extraordinary moral figure the concentration camp victim becomes, a figure realized in such powerful works as those by Primo Levi and Elie Wiesel, that the victim would traverse the boundaries of political manipulation, indeed, transcend politics altogether. This is certainly one effect of the modern cultural and political shaping of the Holocaust in American public debate. "It was the symbol of the survivor – the survivor as emblematic of Jewish suffering, Jewish memory, and Jewish endurance – rather than the highly diverse reality of survivors, that made the greatest contribution to Holocaust commemoration."[37]

This is one reading of the victim who has retained dignity and bearing during the bondage to the camp and continues to do so after liberation. Yet it is one that collapses behind the barbed wire of the extermination camp, precisely because it ignored the "diverse" reality of survivors, where dignity was itself lost. Indeed, Auschwitz was "a microcosmic form of all the evils of the

[36] In the end, this was not the case, as shown in the initial reluctance to commemorate the Holocaust with notable shrines or monuments. For this, see Young, *The Texture of Memory*.

[37] Novick, *The Holocaust and Collective Memory*, 273.

world".[38] Novick notes that the victims, in the name of survival, undertook radical strategies of self-preservation, some of which were ruthless and themselves unforgiving.[39] The psychological portraits of camp inmates by Bruno Bettelheim, himself a survivor of Dachau, spoke of prisoners who were imbued with "regressive" or infantile characteristics, and, in subsequent work, posited the idea of the prisoner who had accepted the total abrogation of freedom, the evisceration of inner feelings to a point of "no return".[40] For Tadeusz Borowski, the victim's world was a moral hell endured on a journey that ultimately ended in the gas chamber, an existence that denuded the sufferer of identity.[41] Giorgio Agamben's commentary on the Holocaust survivor, relying strongly on Levi's works, depicts these figures as existing in a realm which is difficult to reconcile with normal legal or ethical norms.

The camp survivor is a tortured, paradoxical figure that commentators have never fully understood, for to understand it would be to decode Auschwitz. The survivor and Holocaust victim straddle several categories, those of the ethical and the legal, but remain, perversely, a companion to their devil opposites the SS and the Sonderkommando. What Agamben noted in Levi's work was that "Levi succeeded in isolating a new ethical element."[42] Levi offers a useful schema in understanding the debates that were taking place (or in some cases, not taking place) in the United States on the Holocaust, in so far as they demonstrate the complex disservice that was done to the relationship between victims and executioners. His schema proves useful, though his analysis of the camp experience is not taken as conclusive –

---

38 Primo Levi in Conversation with Ian Thomson, in Primo Levi, *The Voice of Memory: Interviews, 1961-1987*, edited by Marco Belponti and Robert Gordon, trans. Robert Gordon (New York: The New Press, 2001), 39.

39 Novick, *The Holocaust and Collective Memory*, 244.

40 Bruno Bettelheim, "Individual and Mass Behaviour in Extreme Situations," *Journal of Abnormal and Social Psychology* 38, 4 (1943): 417-52, 436-7, 444-5; *The Informed Heart: Autonomy in a Mass Age* (Glencoe, Ill: Free Press, 1960), 158; *Surviving, and other Essays* (New York: Alfred A. Knopf, 1979). Bettelheim thereby discusses the concept of the "Muslim" or *Muselmann*, the hollowed out fragment of humanity that Levi regarded as living dead, whose deaths cannot really be called deaths, whose "corpses cannot be called corpses": Giorgio Agamben, *Remnants of Auschwitz: The Witness and the Archive*, trans. Daniel Heller-Roazen (New York: Zone Books, 1999), 70. They are the inmates who were "walking corpses" or "mummy-men": Jean Améry, *At the Mind's Limits: Contemplations by a Survivor on Auschwitz and Its Realities*, trans. Sidney Rosenfeld and Stella O. Rosenfeld (Bloomington: Indiana University Press, 1980), 9; Bettelheim, *Surviving*, 106, A. Carpi, *Diario de Gusen* (Turin: Einaudi, 1993), 17. These points are discussed in Levi, *Remnants of Auschwitz*, 54.

41 Tadeusz Borowski, *This Way for the Gas, Ladies and Gentlemen, and other Stories*, trans. Barbara Vedder (New York: Penguin Books, 1976).

42 Agamben, *Remnants of Auschwitz*, 21.

Levi, for instance, preferred to forgive rather than remain vengeful. It is useful to keep his comments in mind as this inquiry unfolds into political debates on the Final Solution, thereby throwing the contradictions of such discourses into stark relief.

Levi's work manages to give us a framework for evaluating "responsibility", what is termed the "grey zone" where an "incessant alchemy in which good and evil and, along with them, all the metals of traditional ethics reach their point of fusion."[43] The introduction of this grey zone into the discourse is an effective way of contrasting the various approaches taken in American political attitudes to the Holocaust in debates on Germany and Israel. It explains the moral appeal of the Eichmann case to some Americans, for it took the executioner into a different world, one where he could not be resocialized or be rendered benign, thereby placing him alongside his victims, who were represented through the legal offices of the State of Israel.[44]

In the Levian world, the issue of judgment becomes impossible, even if Eichmann is judged. Such a case is never truly closed. There is punishment, but there can never be a punishment suitable for crimes of such magnitude. There are certain parallels in some arguments, both in the discourse on Bitburg, and that of the Eichmann trial, on this notion of responsibility. Either it collapses (as in Bitburg) into a reductionist thesis on alliances and totalitarian simplicity, where the politics of victims and executioners become exchangeable symbols (fascist for communist, Jewish victim for Afghan victim), or the victims become moral punishers. For Eichmann, it is very much a case where a zone of "irresponsibility" is made, where his execution becomes an act that is reasoned "before good and evil," before the realm of conventional ethics takes hold. Nothing can genuinely atone the deed in this "circle", for "no confession of responsibility will remove us".[45]

Levi's complex rendering of the Holocaust problem illuminates another problem: how the scholarship fails to account for more subtle readings of the victim-executioner relationship. Indeed, on a reading of some key works in the field, the focus on the victim becomes paramount, not because such analysis is necessarily incorrect, but because it seems, on principle, to regard the position of the victim as morally unambiguous. In a significant branch of Holocaust studies, the division comes down to a question of evaluating "evil". The scholarship reveals a division in the treatment of evil: evil is dichotomised,

[43] Agamben, *Remnants of Auschwitz*, 21.

[44] The problems with resocializing the executioner are touched upon in Simon Wiesenthal, *Justice Not Vengeance*, trans. Ewald Osers (London: Weidenfeld & Nicolson, 1989), 79.

[45] Agamben, *Remnants of Auschwitz*, 21.

and one that is resolved by either focusing on the victim at the expense of understanding intentions, or executioners in the name of understanding the source of the victims' suffering. Some scholars make it a point not to consider the executioner. Their focus is instead "solely on the testimonies and histories of the victims."[46] The victims become, in a sense, above interrogation for their predicament is not "understandable"[47] though the mistake of this approach lies in the obvious risk that the victim's plight will itself be forgotten, an act of amnesia in retaliation to the unfathomable.

The historiography thereby finds exceptional victims (and executioners) precisely because it has struggled to interpret the very existence of the Holocaust. Dan Diner, as an example, regards Auschwitz as "a no-man's-land of the mind, a black box of explanation; it sucks in all historiographic attempts at interpretation, is a vacuum taking meaning from outside history."[48] The Holocaust seems to face this dilemma: to demand interpretation, yet remain unfathomable in its moral turns and human predicaments. But in the main, one strain of interpretation in the scholarship of the Holocaust elevates the Jewish victim by conferring a dubious privilege: the special place the executioner reserved for them in ideology. George Kren and Leon Rappaport regard one of the key features of this reservation – the death camp – as iconic of a unique historical event, for "the uniqueness of the Holocaust ... stands out when the focus of inquiry is shifted from historical trends to the level of personal experience."[49]

Some works have attempted to analyse the executioner in some detail. Michael R. Marrus, while taking issue with the classification suggested by Kren and Rappaport, still notes that the Holocaust remained singular in its racial objectives, for the need on the part of those who implemented the executions to render the disappearance of the victim total. In one sense, the entire message of "totality" (total elimination, total erasure) was part of Hitler's message.[50] The other groups who were targeted by the Nazis were not different in so far as they suffered death and brutality as their Jewish

[46] Jennifer L. Geddes, "Banal Evil and Useless Knowledge: Hannah Arendt and Charlotte Delbo on Evil after the Holocaust," *Hypatia* 18, 1 (Winter, 2003): 104-115, 104.

[47] Charles S. Maier, *The Unmasterable Past: History, Holocaust and German National Identity* (Cambridge, MA: Harvard University Press, 1988), 92.

[48] Dan Diner, "Zwischen Aporie und Apologie," in D. Diner, ed., *Ist der Nationalsozialistmus Geschichte? Zu Historisierung und Historikerstreit* (Frankfurt am Main: Fischer, 1987), 62-73, 73; also discussed in Maier, *Unmasterable Past*, 92.

[49] George M. Kren and Leon Rappoport, *The Holocaust and the Crisis of Human Behaviour* (New York, 1980), 3.

[50] Michael R. Marrus, *The Holocaust in History* (Hanover: University Press of New England, 1987), 26.

colleagues, but the executioner's intent was otherwise. "Unlike the case with any other group, and unlike the massacres before or since, *every single one* of the millions of targeted Jews was to be murdered. Eradication was to be total. In principle, no Jew was to escape."[51]

Responsibility is reluctantly accorded to some of the participants, and in some cases, it is disturbingly uneven. A key Holocaust scholar, Lucy Dawidowicz, made such a claim in her 1981 study, excoriating some historians "who do not always turn out to be reliable guides on the recovery of the past."[52] The effects of scholarship that has not conformed to the moral dualism of innocence and guilt, noble victim and evil executioner, have faced controversies in academic circles and publishing houses. This was amply demonstrated by the difficulties Raul Hilberg had to face. While his text on the destruction of European Jews remains a tour de force, he noted in his memoirs the near futile attempts to get it published. Yad Vashem found no value in his work, given its lack of precedents for the "heroic Sabra Jew," while Princeton University Press found fault with the study in the field of "public administration".[53]

The pattern of this scholarship is somewhat different to the evolution of American political and public discourses on the Holocaust, most notably when it comes to debates on how the Final Solution has been framed in America's foreign policy debates and international alliances.

The interpretive framework collapses when one confronts the political strategies and tactical interventions that were undertaken by the United States in the three events in question: the initial war crimes policy towards occupied Germany, the Eichmann trial and the Bitburg debate.

SELECTING EVENTS

The scope of this study is not exhaustive, and the selection of events for study is done purely to analyse the framing of the Holocaust in American public and official discourses, with a particular emphasis on foreign policy debate at various historical junctures – the Holocaust as a modality of politics

[51] Marrus, *Holocaust in History*, 24.

[52] Lucy Dawidowicz, *The Holocaust and the Historians* (Cambridge, MA: Harvard University Press, 1981), 142 ff.

[53] Michael Burleigh, *Ethics and Extermination: Reflections on Nazi Genocide* (Cambridge: Cambridge University Press, 1997), 193. Further reflections can be gathered in Hilberg's own memoirs: R. Hilberg, *Politics of Memory: The Journey of a Holocaust Historian* (Chicago: Ivan R. Dee, 1996).

and law, the Holocaust as a fabrication of the relationship between victim and executioner. Germany provided the ideal forum for clashes between the rights and values of the war criminal and the legacy of those who perished under the Third Reich. Israel, in a sense, the state that manifests the triumph of the persecuted Jews, became a nation that shaped the Holocaust through such events as the Eichmann trial.

Through the trial, the politics of the victim is favoured over that of the executioner. In the United States, the debate raged as to how to juggle both positions, though the majority in time was more inclined to respect the politics invoking the six million dead of the Holocaust against the living executioner in the form of Eichmann.

A review of the literature on the subject of German rehabilitation reveals how the suffering of victims of the Final Solution was not a significant driving force in the policies of the Truman and Eisenhower administrations. The rehabilitation of West Germany in American political rhetoric culminates in the other paradox of Holocaust commemoration: the repackaging of Holocaust memory as a construct of an ordinary type of perpetrator. Such crimes, far from being extraordinary or singularly evil, could be treated within an orthodox framework of probationary principles of resocialization.

Nazi officials charged with offences in some districts were often faced with trial delays, "light penalties or no penalties because of intervening policy changes."[54]

Frank M. Buscher's study illustrated the policy considerations behind the American administrations responsible for the governance of occupied Germany. "After Handy and McCloy's January 1951 clemency decisions, the imprisoned war criminals became a purely political problem", a problem that revolved around "the Allied decision to seek a German contribution to the

[54] John Gimbel, "American Denazification and German Local Politics, 1945-1949: A Case Study in Marburg," *American Political Science Review* 54, 1 (March, 1960): 83-105, 84; "The Artificial Revolution in Germany," 92. His main work can be found in the notable *A German Community Under German Occupation, 1945-52* (Stanford, Calif: Stanford University Press, 1961). Studies at a higher administrative level on the effectiveness (or purported ineffectiveness) of the policy began early: William E. Griffith, "The Denazification Program in the United States Zone in Germany," Unpublished PhD Dissertation, Harvard University, 1950; "Denazification in the U.S. Zone of Germany," *Annals of the American Academy of Political and Social* Science 267 (January, 1950): 68-76, 75; Harold Zink, "The American Denazification Program in Germany," *Journal of Central European Affairs* 6 (October, 1946): 227-40; Lewis J. Edinger, "Post-Totalitarian Leadership: Elites in The German Federal Republic," *American Political Science Review* 54, 1 (March, 1960): 58-82; John H. Herz, "The Fiasco of Denazification in Germany," *Political Science Quarterly* 58, 4 (December, 1948): 569-94.

defense of the West against a possible Soviet attack."[55] Buscher subsequently observed that Washington "sold-out" on its war crimes program, while Bonn "was evidently not interested in justice but only in a political solution to the problem."[56] Europe was bracing itself for the Cold War, and the German problem was as much an issue of rapid rehabilitation in the name of making the Western part immune from the Communist bacillus as it was an issue of punishing convicts.[57] Its resources, her scientists, her agents, were all sought after, despite the dark cloud of war crimes.[58]

The central feature to U.S. and German approaches to those convicted of atrocities was one of political calculation rather than judicial wisdom. It involved an almost cultivated neglect of the victim, an omission concealed by the rhetoric of justice to the convicts. Against this, the continuities between the Third Reich and the Federal Republic should not ignore the significant "ostracism of Nazi ideas" as Norbert Frei has called it, to ensure the stability of the Republic from any future seizures of power.[59] The recent German literature on this point suggests that the politics of the 1950s saw the "integration of former Nazis while at the same time asserting that the political

---

[55] Frank M. Buscher, *The U.S. War Crimes Trial Program in Germany, 1946-1955* (New York: Greenwood Press, 1989), 161; Peter Maguire, *Law and War: An American Story* (New York: Columbia University Press, 2000), 124-5.

[56] Buscher, *The U.S. War Crimes Trial Program in Germany*, 85. Robert Engler, "The Individual Soldier and the Occupation," *Annals of the American Academy of Political and Social Science* 267 (January 1950): 77-86, 79l, John Mendelsohn, "War Crimes Trials and Clemency in Germany and Japan," in Robert Wolfe, ed., *Americans as Proconsuls: United States Military Government in Germany and Japan, 1944-1952* (Carbondale: Carbondale: Southern Illinois University Press, 1984), 226-59.

[57] Marrus, "The Nuremberg Trials," 569; Wolfgang Krieger, "Was General Clay a Revisionist? Strategic Aspects of the United States Occupation of Germany," *Journal of Contemporary History* 18 (1983): 165-84. William Manchester's study on the renowned German industrialist family Krupp also revealed this Cold War framework of values: William R. Manchester, *The Arms of Krupp, 1587-1968* (New York: Bantam Books, 1970); John Gimbel, "The Artificial Revolution in Germany: A Case Study," *Political Science Quarterly* 76, 1 (March, 1961): 88-104, 92; John Gimbel, *A German Community under American Occupation: Marburg, 1945-1952* (Stanford, CA: Stanford University Press, 1961).

[58] Tom Bower, *A Blind Eye to Murder: Britain, America and the Purging of Nazi Germany: A Pledge Betrayed* (London: Andrew Deutsch, 1981); and see Christopher Simpson, *Blowback: America's Recruitment of Nazis and its Effect on the Cold War (*New York: MacMillan, 1988). For the more specific use of German science by the Allied forces, tainted by slave labour and atrocities, see Bower's *The Paperclip Conspiracy: The Battle for the Spoils and Science of Nazi Germany* (London: M. Joseph/Rainbird, 1987). Japan also provided similar instances of clemency in the name of scientific usefulness: Peter Williams and David Wallace, *Unit 731: Japan's Secret Biological Warfare in World War II* (New York: Free Press, 1989), in particular Chapters 11, 12.

[59] Norbert Frei, *Karrieren im Zwielicht. Hitler's Eliten nach 1945* (Frankfurt: Campus Verlag, 2001), 129.

and economic constitution of the Federal Republic was the negation of National Socialism."[60]

This does not, however, override the substantive manipulation and politicisation of the war criminal issue that Frei documents with clarity in his landmark work on Chancellor Konrad Adenauer's response to de-nazification. Such writing rests comfortably with Buscher and Maguire's work on the contradictory American responses on the subject.[61] What is significant is that all these studies reveal that the early years of the Federal Republic saw "concerns for the victims of Nazism [take] a back seat in contrast to the a widespread solidarity with other former members of the Nazi *Volksgemeinschaft*, even if they were deeply implicated in the regime's crimes."[62] The focus of "the policy for the past" was less on Nazism's victims and more on "those considered 'victims' of its overcoming" leading to "ersatz enactments of a politically corrupted but nonetheless still virulent nationalism that Adenauer had effectively forbidden the Germans."[63] One could therefore be forgiven for thinking that such a policy led to a demarcation of guilt and history, a "symbolic" exoneration of past crimes.[64]

On the Bitburg ceremony, the literature remains divided. Hagiography occupies one extreme of the spectrum; revulsion the other. We see a different view of the Holocaust at play, one where the perpetrators were subtly exculpated, their contributions to the war acknowledged in a ceremony that arose out of a "public relations" that "was perfectly calculated to appeal to Reagan's Christian notions of forgiveness and rebirth."[65] Bitburg demonstrated the shocked realisation that they were two operative visions of the Holocaust in separate discursive spaces, an Americanized Holocaust that could not be reduced to strategic goals and interrogation, and a quite different Holocaust, amenable to strategic use, easily adapted for the rhetoric of

---

[60] Helmut König, *Die Zukunft der Vergangenheit. Der Nationalsozialismus im politischen Bewußtein der Bundesrepublik* (Frankfurt am Main: Fischer Taschenbuch, 2003), 25.

[61] Norbert Frei, *Adenauer's Germany and the Nazi Past. The Politics of Amnesty and Integration*, trans. Joel Golb (New York: Columbia University Press, 2002), from the original *Vergangenheitspolitik: Die Anfänge der Bundesrepublik und die NS-Vergangenheit* (Munich: Beck, 1996). For the influence of his work, see summary in Kay Schiller, "The Presence of the Nazi Past in the Early Decades of the Bonn Republic," *Journal of Contemporary History* 39, 2 (April, 2004): 285-294, 286.

[62] Schiller, "The Presence of the Nazi Past," 288.

[63] Frei, *Adenauer's Germany*, xii, 308.

[64] Frei, *Adenauer's Germany*, xiii. See also Frank Biess, "Between Amnesty and Anti-Communism: The West German *Kameradenschinder* Trials, 1948-1960," in Omer Bartov, Atina Grossman and Mary Nolan, eds., *Crimes of War: Guilt and Denial in the Twentieth Century* (New York: The New Press, 2002), 138-160.

[65] Edmund Morris, *Dutch: A Memoir of Ronald Reagan* (New York: Random House, 1999), 514.

forgiveness in foreign relations. The U.S. political debate favouring reconciliation instead focused on new executioners and victims: the oppressed behind the Iron curtain and perceived dangers of totalitarian communism in the Americas and Afghanistan.[66]

Reagan's reading of the Holocaust within the framework of the U.S.-German relationship, one based on forgiveness and strategic considerations, was heavily disputed. Forgotten was the fact "that the German army [was] itself an active and willing participant in the Holocaust."[67] In the view of a scholar specialising in the readings of German philosopher Jürgen Harbermas: "That Reagan would hope to visit Bergen-Belsen concentration camp and Bitburg on the same day, satisfying equally the memory of victims suffered by all sides, betrays either his naivete or his stupidity, and likely both."[68] Prominent American academic Geoffrey Hartman argued that Reagan "compounded his error [at Bitburg] by explanatory statements that made no distinction between the fallen German soldiers and the murdered Jews". Warriors in crime became victims; and the crimes of World War II became the progeny of "one man".[69] The writings on this score protest against the amalgamation of positions: the moral path of the executioner and that of the victim could never meet on the plane of public relations and political kitsch.[70]

The American discourses surrounding the Eichmann trial interrogated the legacies of the Final Solution, promoting its relevance to Americans while revealing a conflict with the official war crimes discourse that had been employed towards Germany.[71] The literature on the Eichmann case can also be realized as a conflict of the victim-executioner, with the politics of the victim triumphing.[72] It was, in the words of Israeli philosopher and author Boaz

---

66 For examples, see "Voting on Bitburg," *National Review* 37 (May 31, 1985): 12-13; "Satanic Force v Evil Empire," *National Review* 37 (May 31, 1985): 13; William F. Buckley, "Inquest," *National Review* 37 (June 14, 1985): 54.

67 Daniel Goldhagan, "A Bitburg Foonote: The German Army and the Holocaust," *New Republic* 192, 20 (May 13, 1985): 13-4, 13. Goldhagen would subsequently write his controversial work on the same theme in *Hitler's Willing Executioners: Ordinary Germans and the Holocaust* (New York: Alfred A. Knopf, 1996).

68 Martin Beck Matustik, *Jürgen Harbermas: Philosophical-Political Life* (Lanham: Rowman & Littlefield Publishers, Inc., 2001), 76.

69 Hartman, *The Longest Shadow*, 65.

70 Midge Decter, "Bitburg: Who Forgot What," *Commentary* 80 (August, 1985): 21-7; Peter Marin, "Words, for the President, Upon Laying a Wreath," *Harper's* 271 (July, 1985): 11-12; Kenneth S. Kantzer, "Bitburg: Must We Forgive?" *Christianity Today* 29 (July 12, 1985): 14-15.

71 On the effect of the trial, see Harold E. Quinley and Charles Y. Glock, *Anti-Semitism in America* (New York: Free Press, 1979), 114.

72 See Tom Segev, *The Seventh Million: The Israelis and the Holocaust* (New York: Hill & Wang, 1993); and see the debate in Prima Lahav, *Judgment in Jerusalem: Chief Justice*

Evron, announced "to the world that such crimes will not go unpunished, and [made] Israel instrumental in the application of the highest principles of human justice and international law".[73] American political arguments in general saw Israel as the appropriate judge, thereby providing the final realisation of justice for Holocaust victims by vesting them with "semantic authority".[74]

Any attempt to challenge this progression of Holocaust discourse towards archetypal evil and meek noble suffering was challenged, most notably in the controversy surrounding the Arendt debate.[75] As one American review of Hannah Arendt's *Eichmann in Jerusalem* suggested, the trial managed to confuse "the traditional distinction between the traditional sufferings of the Jews and the entirely new meaning of crimes against the human status." Implicit in the critique was the suggestion that genocide and Eichmann's crimes were an international cause of concern, and to bring the notion of identity into the crimes was to confuse Nuremberg's fundamental assertion of "crimes against humanity" with notions of "folktale justice".[76] This criticism tended to overlook the converse: the application of crimes against humanity by its nature tended to subsume the Holocaust into a broader and more general narrative of human criminality.

Simon Agranat and the Zionist Century (Berkeley, CA: University of California Press, 1997), 145-165, and the good discussion in H. Rosenberg, "The Trial and Eichmann," *Commentary* 32, 5 (May, 1961): 369-81. For objections on legal and moral grounds to his trial, see Yosal Rogat, *The Eichmann Trial and the Rule of Law* (Santa Barbara, Calif.: Center for the Study of Democratic Institutions, Fund for the Republic, November 1961); "Eichmann the Christian?" *America* 106 (March 24, 1962): 814-5; Robert K. Woetzel, *The Nuremberg Trials in International Law with a Postlude on the Eichmann Case* (New York: Frederick A. Praeger, Inc., 1962), 258; Victor Gollancz, "The Case of Adolph Eichmann," *Minnesota Review* 3, 2 (Winter, 1963): 257-262; Milton Mayer, "Eichmann in Israel," *The Progressive* 25 (April, 1961): 17-20. See the discussion between Arthur Gilbert and Walter M. Abbott, "Christians Failed Jewish Hopes," *America* 106 (March 24, 1962): 825-8.

[73] Evron, "Holocaust," 12.

[74] Michael A. Musmano, "The Objections Intimine to the Eichmann Trial," *Temple Law Quarterly* 35, 1 (Fall 1961): 1-22; Russell J. Weintraub, "Does Israel Have Jurisdiction Over Eichmann?" *National Jewish Monthly* 75, 8 (April, 1961): 5, 32-4, 5; Helen Silving, "In Re Eichmann: A Dilemma of Law and Morality," *The American Journal of International Law* 55 (1961): 307-58, 336. See also 308, 330-1; Shoshana Felman, "Theatres of Justice: Arendt in Jerusalem, the Eichmann Trial, and the Redefinition of Legal Meaning in the Wake of the Holocaust," *Critical Inquiry* 27 (Winter, 2001): 201-238, 233, 221.

[75] The scathing work in criticism of Arendt was Jacob Robinson, *And the Crooked Shall be Made Straight* (New York: Macmillan, 1965).

[76] Ronald Berman, "Hostis Humani Generis," Review of Eichmann in Jerusalem, *Kenyon Review* (Summer, 1963): 541-6, 541; Benjamin Robinson, "The Specialist in the Eichmann Precedent: Morality and Law and Military Sovereignty," *Critical Inquiry* 30, 1 (Autumn, 2003): 63-97.

The result of this inadvertently de-radicalised the Holocaust, returning it to the fold of Nuremberg's rhetoric of civilizational punishment.[77]

FORGIVENESS FROM THIRD PARTIES

The politics of the victim and executioner, at least as appraised by the American political establishment, proved flexible in the practice of foreign policy.

Guilt could be modified; forgiveness to infractions extended when needed. Such an approach tends to make a mockery of the ethical complexities that govern the relationship between victim and executioner, which is the implication of Levi's ethical "grey zone." The grey zone traps participants in a context where, "Victim and executioner are equally ignoble; the lesson of the camps is brother in abjection."[78] They are both left in a land where orthodoxies in ethics are no longer comprehensible, and should be left there.

A note here is required as to why the issue of forgiveness should even arise, given its seemingly inappropriate place in discussions about Jewish suffering.[79] This is largely due to the fact that debates about the Holocaust in the United States employed forgiveness in their lexicon, effectively "Christianising" the debate.

This was most stark in the debates surrounding the Eichmann trial, when such prominent journals as *America* regarded the death penalty as gratuitous and Israel's reluctance to forgive a serious error of judgment. It also issued in most spectacular fashion from the Kohl-Reagan gathering at the Bitburg ceremony in 1985.

Nor has the issue of Christian symbolism been entirely alien to the publicising of the Holocaust legacy. Publicists of Holocaust debate have not been averse to employing the semiology of Christian themes, most notably on the note of redemption – at least for the victims. Certainly, there is some

---

[77] Such a problem was touched upon by the Israeli Justice Simon Agranat, who attempted to solve the conflict by framing Eichmann's crimes within the normative framework of international law, deflecting criticisms of the extra-legal nature of Eichmann's apprehension. His crimes were "acts which damage vital international interests," whilst also revolting universal notions of an "enlightened humanity": Agranat, cited in Lahav, *Judgment in Jerusalem*, 154.

[78] Primo Levi, *Conversazioni e interviste* (Turin: Einaudi, 1997), 216 and noted in Agamben, *Remnants of Auschwitz*, 17.

[79] A discussion is available in Richard Harries, *After the Evil: Christianity and Judaism in the Shadow of the Holocaust* (Oxford: Oxford University Press, 2003), 65 ff.

comment on how Wiesel as "the emblematic survivor" in time "cultivated [a] persona as symbol of suffering," a Christ-like immanence that has been noted by his Jewish critics.[80]

The relationship between victim and executioner is rendered even more problematic by the Nuremberg trials. The United States and its Allies created a space of legal judgment and absolution, assuming the power to judge and redress grievances inflicted by German authorities on German and non-German subjects. With such an assumption came the power to alter the legal-political relationship of executioners vis-à-vis their victims. This suggested an assumption of sovereignty, that which "consists in the fact that the sovereign is, at the same time, outside and inside the juridical order."[81] Harsh sentences could be changed, which is exactly what the US Review Boards that subsequently dealt with parole applications did. Even if the German convicts at Landsberg and other U.S. prisons had been responsible for the deaths of Jews, their crimes proved to be no barrier to the favourable treatment they subsequently received in the U.S. zone of occupation. This gave the impression that decisions affecting their welfare were not made in the name of their victims. They were made in the name of Cold War alliances, in the name of Adenauer's public relations and a stable West Germany.

The significance of the legal framing of the Holocaust by the Nuremberg trials lay in its generality, a crime against all humans rather than one specifically against Jews.

The rhetoric of the U.S. prosecution at Nuremberg would amply demonstrate this. Mass criminality was a matter of civilization, where the specifics of victim identity (ethnicity, religion) proved less important than the status of humanity itself. As Norbert Elias observed in his elaboration of the "civilizing process", civilization down plays "the national differences between peoples; it emphasises what is common to all human beings or – in the view of its bearers – should be."[82]

The most obvious contrast is *Kultur*, where the stress is on difference, where the boundaries of identity are renewed, and redefinitions sought. The punishment of war criminals served as a purging of the uncommon, the aberrations of human behaviour, but the victims were treated as common holders of the same fate, sharing the same suffering at the hand of all fascists.

---

[80] Novick, *The Holocaust and Collective Memory*, 274.

[81] Giorgio Agamben, *Homo Sacer: Sovereign Power and a Bare Life*, trans. Daniel Heller-Roazen (Stanford, CA: Stanford University Press, 1998), 15.

[82] Norbert Elias, *The Civilizing Process: Sociogenetic and Psychogenetic Investigations*, trans. Edmund Jephcott, Rev. Edition (Oxford: Blackwell Publishers, 2000), 7.

A demonstration of how slippery the moral ground of Holocaust politics is in American foreign policy was amply demonstrated in the sham display of forgiveness at Bitburg. The juggling consideration was sovereignty, which remains inseparable from the act of forgiveness, even in today's practice of humanitarianism.[83] President Reagan with Chancellor Helmut Kohl, moving through a cemetery, dramatised a process of forgiveness. But it was the making of a bold claim: the power to forgive, which was assumed despite Wiesel's contentions to the contrary. Do not, he warned, go there, for you do not belong there. As Jacques Derrida suggests, each act of forgiveness assumes the existence of a "sovereign power." True forgiveness is only possible when it is "unconditional but without sovereignty."[84]

That remains an ideal. American political appraisals of the Holocaust, at least when it came to Washington's relationship with Germany, refused to accept the "secret" and "inaccessible" zone of experience for the victim beyond juridical and political principles.[85] The secret of the victim's trauma was not accepted. Initially, it was exposed at Nuremberg in grand trials that were not held in the name of Jewish victims. It was then ignored in the name of convict welfare and political expediency. The Holocaust assumed a politico-juridical form, where victims compete for recognition (Eichmann and Israel; Bitburg), or face a struggle against the ascendancy of the executioner in Cold War political strategies, strategies that ultimately arose at Bitburg as a staged reconciliation between old foes against a common enemy: Soviet communism.

The issue of forgiveness is itself a problematic one, and open to dispute. Forgiveness, argues Derrida, is equivocal, often "confounded, sometimes in calculated fashion, with related themes: excuse, regret, amnesty, prescription, etc.; so many significations of which come under law, a penal law which forgives must in principle remain heterogeneous and irreducible." An event such as Nuremberg, in its claim to punish crimes against humanity, remained "on the horizon of the entire geopolitics of forgiveness."[86] The legal spectacles staged by the various Clemency Boards of the U.S. occupation forces were of such geopolitical import, focusing on an ominous future, where Bolshevism became infused with Nazi traits. As the keen student of totalitarianism Claude Lefort noted, "communism [during the Cold War] was defined as a totalitarian

---

[83] Jacques Derrida, *On Cosmopolitanism and Forgiveness*, trans. Michael Hughes and M. Dooley (Routledge: London, 2001), 58.
[84] Derrida, *On Cosmopolitanism and Forgiveness*, 59.
[85] These terms are from Derrida, *On Cosmopolitanism and Forgiveness*, 55.
[86] Derrida, *On Cosmopolitanism and Forgiveness*, 31.

system, the most highly developed and perfected example of that system, one which had withstood the destruction of fascism and national socialism, but which proceeded from the same causes and pursued similar ends." Communism was invested with "features which had once been imputed to fascism."[87] In the context of this inquiry, the issue of forgiveness is an analytical tool that helps to understand an aspect of US policy towards the Holocaust in the German theatre.

Derrida further chooses to distinguish between a sentence that punishes and the notion of forgiveness. One is not the correlative of the other; a prisoner can be kept in prison with a harsh sentence and still be forgiven; the same prisoner might be released and yet remain unforgiven.[88] This observation has some value, but it need not stand up to the practical outcomes of the case. Why would the forgiven languish in prison, or those released early in their sentence remain unforgiven?

The political discourse in U.S. and German circles that took place on the issue of the Federal Republic's involvement in European defence emphasized the executioner's heroic valour, or the particular values in fighting off communism.

Heroism was regarded as inconsistent with the war crime label; indeed the only war criminals, argued many Germans even after defeat, were those in the Allied occupation forces. As for the Jews, they simply never asked on the issue of forgiveness.

In reality, the point of such an event as the Holocaust, or Shoah, is that forgiveness remains an issue of dispute, whatever forms of national or geopolitical therapy are applied to it.

The point is made by Jankélévitch when he asserts that, "Forgiveness died in the death camps." The Shoah never presented an issue of forgiveness because, unlike the SS soldier in *The Sunflower*, the criminals never asked forgiveness.[89]

He goes further, suggesting that a crime against humanity cannot be forgiven at all, since it constitutes a crime against what it is to be a person. But in his earlier writing (for instance, *Le Pardon*) he leaves room for the suggestion that forgiveness is possible provided it occurs in the realm of "hyperbolic ethics," an ethics that exists beyond ethics, which reads as an

[87] Claude Lefort, *The Political Forms of Modern Society: Bureaucracy, Democracy, Totalitarianism*, trans. John B. Thompson (Cambridge: Polity Press, 1986), 274.

[88] Derrida, *Cosmopolitanism and Forgiveness*, 33.

[89] Jankélévitch makes this point in an essay 'L'Imprescriptible' which Derrida discusses: *Cosmopolitanism and Forgiveness*, 34.

approximation to Levy's ethical realm of victim-executioner.[90] Levi prefers to be forgiving. Too much, he argued, was written by those who had never understood those "depths of human degradation. Those who did not come back and tell the tale."[91]

The point of the discussion ultimately does not turn on whether Derrida's view of forgiveness or that of Jankélévitch's is to prevail; what matters is how the Holocaust was framed in these official and public debates in America, and how they represented the politics of executioner and victim. The actions of the U.S. administration in Germany intrude upon the terrain of Holocaust morality through affecting the asymmetrical morality between victim and executioner. Punishment, as Arendt noted, "has something in common with forgiveness, as it tends to put a limit on something that without intervention could continue indefinitely."[92] The result of American punishments therefore provided a therapy of forgiveness (even if it was never true or unconditional), a feature realized with force during the Bitburg ceremonies. The outrage that arose had as much to do with this revelation of appropriation of the Shoah by non-Jews in assuming that such juridical intervention after World War II could mitigate guilt through an ethics of forgiveness. In the end, if there was to be forgiveness, it could only be in "hyperbolic" ethics, in a new world beyond ethics, and ultimately, between the victim and executioner.

---

[90] Derrida, *Cosmopolitanism and Forgiveness*, 36.
[91] Levi, with Thomson, in *The Voice of Memory*, 41.
[92] Quoted in Derrida, *Cosmopolitanism and Forgiveness*, 37.

Chapter 2

THE POLITICS OF THE EXECUTIONER

DEBATING THE FINAL SOLUTION AND GERMANY, 1946-1960

> Meanwhile the Germans, untroubled by regret – because after all they did nothing wrong, they only did what they were supposed to do – keep on saying with energy: we are not Nazis. It is their idea of the password to forgiveness, probably followed by a sizeable loan.
>
> Martha Gellhorn, *The Face of War*, 162.

Simon Wiesenthal ends his study of evil and forgiveness in *The Sunflower* by being less than forthcoming with the latter. The SS man asks to be forgiven for his crimes against humanity. To that end, Wiesenthal refuses. His contemporaries in a symposium at the end of the work differ in their opinions. Their discussions are emblematic of the dilemma of how the Holocaust was framed at certain historical junctures in U.S. public and foreign policy discourse. Was it an important memory to be juggled with conscience and guilt, or a matter to be condemned to amnesia by acts of amnesty and forgiveness? This was certainly important in the context of the emerging Cold War rivalries, where old and mortal enemies would have to become new friends. *The Sunflower* provides a crucial interpretation of the dynamics between the executioner and the victim, their political and ethical roles.[93] Do

[93] Simon Wiesenthal, *The Sunflower, with a Symposium* (New York: Schocken Books, 1976).

not forgive someone in the position of the SS man, wrote Herbert Marcuse, because that very act perpetuates the crime, an act as cynical as the gesture of an assassin's mother who comforts the mother whose child has been murdered. It was "inhuman and a travesty of justice if the executioner asked the victim to forgive."[94] Kurt von Schuschnigg, despite his Christian feelings, saw this as pernicious: only God could grant such an order; to do otherwise was dishonest.[95] For Manès Sperber, the grant of a pardon "before you are certain that the guilty on their side will always remember their guilt" was nothing more than "a continuance of their crime."[96]

These debates provide a backdrop where the politics of Holocaust and war crimes discourse was first historically situated. In the closing stages of the Second World War, forgiveness or empathy for the executioners was scarce. American soldiers witnessed those Buchenwald warriors who charged off aimlessly after their liberation, a "crack" regiment of inmates that had just journeyed from the camp in search of a vengeful victory against their murderous captors.[97] There were spontaneous bursts of violence against the SS and the camp guards. General Hobart Gay after witnessing Buchenwald professed the attitudes of many an Allied soldier as the camps were being liberated: "No race except a people dominated by an ideology of sadism could have committed such gruesome crimes [...] To take prisoners out and shoot them is kind, but to deliberately starve them to death is an atrocity." Politicians who had "criticized minor events of alleged cruelty on the part of American soldiers" would no doubt "frantically preach to people that the Germans are grand people, and that they should be given our love and munificent gratitude."[98]

In contrast, the liberated *Muselmann* and other concentration camp inmates were initially revered as specimens of supreme survival, initially accorded singular moral status. Jean Améry described his experience after surviving Auschwitz in such a manner. The liberated victim of German brutality was a political pop star with dazzling moral worth. "[F]or quite sometime there lasted what was for me totally unprecedented social and moral status, and it elated me to the extreme: being what I was – a surviving

[94] Marcuse was referring to the murder of the Weimar Republic's important figure, Rathenau: *Sunflower Symposium*, in Wiesenthal, *The Sunflower*, 169.

[95] *Sunflower Symposium* in Wiesenthal, *The Sunflower*, 201.

[96] *Sunflower Symposium*, in Wiesenthal, *The Sunflower*, 205.

[97] This is recorded in RG 319, National Archives, Maryland Branch, and noted in David Hackett, ed., *The Buchenwald Report* (Boulder, Colorado: University of Colorado, 1995).

[98] Gay's impressions were presumably from April 15, 1945 in Blumenthal, ed., *The Patton Papers*, II, 687.

Resistance fighter, Jew, victim of persecution by a universally hated regime – there was mutual understanding between me and the rest of the world [...] I was in tune with public opinion that surrounded me."[99]

The spectacle of the Nuremberg war crimes trials continues to mould the victim narrative, but adopts the tenor of universalism. Robert Jackson's address for the U.S. prosecution as chief advocate at the Nuremberg Trials charged the Nazis with crimes against ethnic groups under the more general category of crimes against humanity. "The most savage and numerous crimes planned and committed by the Nazis were those against the Jews. These in Germany, in 1933, numbered about 500,000. In the aggregate, they had made for themselves positions which excited envy, and had accumulated properties which excited the avarice of the Nazis. They were few enough to be helpless and numerous enough to be held up as a menace." Jackson made it a primary objective in the U.S. prosecution case to "to show a plan and design, to which all Nazis were fanatically committed, to annihilate all Jewish people."[100]

Améry's post-liberation euphoria and the publicised moral exceptionality of the Holocaust survivor proved short lived. The treatment of Germany's war criminals by successive U.S. administrations through the late 1940s and the early 1950s ushered in a new phase of attitudes towards the Holocaust. Towards the international community, officials and public personalities in the United States expressed shock at the crimes that had been exposed at the concentration camps. But this attitude did not necessarily prevail in the appraisal of America's strategic interests. New allies were needed in the forthcoming battles against global communism and the battles of the Cold War. To this end, punitive approaches towards Germany, such as the controversial de-industrialising premise of the Morgenthau Plan, were not only frowned upon but rejected.[101]

The politics of nation states eschewed notions such as the immemorial nature of individual political crimes: states were themselves above crimes,

---

[99] Améry, *At the Mind's Limits*, 64-5.

[100] Robert Jackson, Opening Address for the US Prosecution, printed in *Nazi Conspiracy & Aggression*, Volume I, Chapter VII, Office of the United States Chief Counsel for Prosecution of Axis Criminality (United States Government Printing Office, Washington, D.C., 1946), 135.

[101] The plan was defeated, and the Treasury Department estranged from the other bureaucracies in Washington. In a review published in *Commentary*, one author claimed that Morgenthau "may seriously fail to recognise [what similarity] his 'solution' has to Nazi technique": Guenter Reimann, "Should Germany Be Ruralized?" *Commentary* 1, 3 (January, 1946): 90-1, 91. See also Memorandum by Chief of Division of Central European Affairs (Riddleberger), Washington, January 15, 1945, *Foreign Relations of the United States*, 1945: III, 388-9, 389 (herein *FRUS*).

even if they issued rhetorical statements on the legitimacy of punishing its leaders.[102] Ironically, when so prominent a figure at Nuremberg as Justice Jackson repudiated the notion that sovereignty is not infinite when it comes to committing crimes, he left room for the implication that sovereignty is very much infinite when it comes to forgiving and punishing those crimes. The politics of the perpetrator was revealed as a juggle of variables: horse-trading on security, rearming Germany, and war criminal welfare in the name of American ideals of justice. In time the Holocaust victims (both dead and living) were humanitarian signposts to be bypassed. As Henry Greenspan writes, "The world and public opinion moved on. Améry was left with what he said the experience had always been at its core: 'an extreme loneliness.'"[103] The acceleration of Cold War hostilities and the paramount interest in stabilising Germany again, as in 1919, figured in the calculations of the American administration.[104] Then Secretary of State Robert Lansing was less interested in punishing the Kaiser for war crimes than other contesting considerations of political stability. He saw that a stable Germany would act as a bulwark against the Bolshevik contagion in the east. "We have seen the hideous consequences of Bolshevik rule in Russia, and we know that the doctrine is spreading westward."

Lansing emphasized the need to dilute the atrocity when broader state interests required it: "We must look to the future, even though we forget the immediate demands of justice."[105] While justice and punishment were desirable, "The question [was] much greater than that."[106] Notwithstanding the inroads made into state sovereignty by the Nuremberg trials, Realpolitik remained significant in framing American political discourses on the Holocaust, reflecting Carl Schmitt's view that politics can never "be made safe" from antagonistic tendencies.[107]

---

[102] To this end, it is instructive to compare Jackson's commentary of the Nuremberg trial as penetrating the veil of sovereignty, to his position on not trying industrialists in a second trial: see Donald Bloxham, "The Trial That Never Was: Why there was no Second International Trial of Major War Criminals at Nuremberg," *History: The Journal of the Historical Association* 87, 285 (January 2002): 41-60.

[103] Henry Greenspan, "'An Immediate and Violent Impulse': Holocaust Survivor Testimony in the First Years After Liberation," in John K. Roth and Elisabeth Maxwell, eds., *Remembering for the Future: The Holocaust in an Age of Genocide* (Hampshire: Palgrave, 2001), III: Memory, 108-116, 110.

[104] For accounts of this, see Maguire, *Law and* War, 78.

[105] Lansing on May 8, 1919, quoted in Maguire, *Law and War*, 78.

[106] Letter to Edward N. Smith, November 14, 1918, Lansing Papers, cited in James Morgan Read, *Atrocity Propaganda* (New York: Arno Press, 1972), 256.

[107] Carl Schmitt, *The Concept of the Political*, trans. George Schwab (Chicago: University of Chicago Press, 1996), xiv-xv.

Indeed, when it comes to Nuremberg, where crimes against Jews were publicly noted for the first time, the legal relevance of its proceedings were openly questioned both during and after its deliberations. The manner of framing such laws proved problematic for the concept of a specific victim status. All victims of atrocities were classed as victims of crimes against humanity. The American Review Boards could therefore issue pardons, parole orders and lesser periods of incarceration because they referred to general laws of humanity (not specific crimes of ethnicity). They could issue pardons in the name of American jurisprudence, which was as much a pardon on crimes that were also committed against their own soldiers. Such generalised legal approaches overlooked the specific nature of Jewish suffering which led, in time, to modifications and strategic changes in the war crimes programme.

The jurisprudential legacy of punishing in the name of the victim suffered. Somewhat opportunely, as the clemency board was handing down a spate of generous rulings, a committee of the American Society of International Law claimed in its proceedings that "few distinguishable rules of the law of war" still existed despite the decisions of the International Military Tribunal.[108] The assault on the legacy of Nuremberg would continue through to the 1960s.[109]

The result was a peculiar distortion of attitudes to the Holocaust in American political debates in the earlier part of the Cold War. Such attitudes projected confidence and leniency, taking alliances seriously in rehabilitating Germany.

The Nuremberg trials suffered from these antinomies of justice and Holocaust memory. It issued, not from the vengeance of Holocaust survivors, but the victors of the Second World War. A great "historical tragedy" as one commentator wrote in a column at the time of the Eichmann trial, was that "after the war, the Nazi criminals were not judged by their own victims."[110]

A cardinal aspect to this historical tragedy was the specific approach of American penology. It duly placed the welfare of executioners at the forefront, disregarding victims and the need for substantial retributive punishment. This is not to say that severe sentences were not handed down, nor executions avoided – examples were provided by the executions of figures of such

[108] *Proceedings of the American Society of International Law* 46 (1952), 218, cited in Guenter Lewy, "Superior Orders, Nuclear Warfare, and the Dictates of Conscience: The Dilemma of Military Obedience in the Atomic Age," *American Political Science Review* 55, 1 (March 1961): 3-23, 3.

[109] For this, see William J. Bosch, *Judgment on Nuremberg: American attitudes towards the Major German War Crime Trials* (Chapel Hill: University of Carolina Press, 1970).

[110] F. Lohenbill, "The Disgrace of the Eichmann Trial," *Contemporary Issues* 48 (Spring 1964): 9-10, 9.

notoriety as Otto Ohlendorf.[111] These, however, remained unusual. Only four of the initial fourteen death sentences handed down in the Einzatzgruppen Case were upheld.[112]

Importantly, the discussion of memory – those centred on past atrocities – assumed a secondary place. This may have also had something to do with the framing of the charges at the trials.

American policies on war crimes signalled a universalizing trend towards atrocity, suggested by the charge of "crimes against humanity", a concept that overlooked the more complex nuances of the victim, or at least the specific circumstances of suffering, in preference for a civilizational cure.

The legal proceedings were themselves notable for the mention of ethnic crime as a subset of crimes against humanity, the trials being a grand purging of an aberration of civilization rather than a reverential gesture to specific victims. Regarding the specific case of Dr. Werner Braune, who was charged with "crimes against humanity," the closing brief of the U.S. Counsel noted how, "The crimes set forth in the bill of particular under this Count of Indictment were part and parcel of the over-all plan and policy of the National Socialist State to destroy foreign races and ethnic groups by murder."[113] Jews constituted a miscellany of victims who had suffered at the hands of totalitarianism.

The closing arguments additionally noted "the slaughter of 800 gypsies and insane people to ensure the security of the fighting forces."[114]

The U.S. prosecution in the Ohlendorf case similarly highlighted "crimes against humanity" rather than a more specifmic race-based atrocity: "The Prosecution respectfully submits that Otto Ohlendorf ordered, aided, abetted and took consenting part in the crimes of murder, spoilation of property, persecution on political, racial and religious grounds, against Russian Nationals."[115]

The Jewish victims therefore took a less than dignified second place. The mechanism of retribution established through the tribunal system failed to

---

[111] John J. McCloy and General Hardy, "Execution of Landsberg Criminal War Criminals," Released to Press, June 7, *Department of State Bulletin* 24 (June 18, 1951): 988.

[112] "Landsberg: A Documentary Report," January 31, 1951, HICOG, Papers of John. J.McCloy, RG 466, Classified General Records 1949-1952, D(51) 123, NARA, CP, MD.

[113] Military Tribunal No. II, Case No. 9, "Closing Brief For the United States of America Against Werner Braune," Numberg, January 1948, 1; in Mendelsohn, ed., *The Holocaust*, vol. 18, 2.

[114] Military Tribunal No. II, Case No. 9, "Closing Brief," 2, in Mendelsohn, ed., *The Holocaust*, 2.

[115] Submission of P. W. Walton, Military Tribunal No. II, Case No. IX, "Closing Brief For the United States of America against Otto Ohlendorf," Numberg, 1948, 16, extracted in Mendelsohn, ed., *The Holocaust*, vol. 18, 89.

restore their position in history.[116] The policy of the American forces was concerned with sentences that masked the enormity of unconventional crimes, and sentences which, once rendered conventional, could be diminished or modified by parole or clemency.

SHIFTING RATIONALES: SHOCK

The story of American official debate on the subject of the Holocaust in Germany is one of extremes. The first reactions to the Final Solution[117] can be gathered from the accounts noted in the *Buchenwald Report* and those of prominent figures who sought to discuss their experiences for the American public back home.[118] These accounts set the scene for a brief, intense burst of speculation on the nature of the German executioner and his unfortunate victims. A particularly rich source of material on the nature of the concentration camp system were private agents who provided a series of gory descriptions to their superiors. A captured Roger Lanze, who was in Dachau, wrote a report to the Office of Strategic Services on the hysterically cruel spectacle of spitting women and vicious dogs, and various pastimes of the executioners. "One of the favourite distractions of the SS consisted of throwing a Jewish or Communist prisoner into the concrete mixers while he was still living. The man was crushed to death and poured out with the concrete."[119]

The newly liberating U.S. forces were keen to record the repellent scenes of misery that were unfolding, including those of surviving Jews.[120] General Dwight D. Eisenhower was, despite the sanguinary spectacle of Buchenwald,

---

[116] The philosophy of retributive punishment and its role in "restoring" the victim is discussed in M. Minow, *Between Vengeance and Forgiveness: Facing History after Genocide and Mass Violence* (Boston: Beacon Press, 1998), 12-3.

[117] Importantly, it has to be noted that the perception of any Final Solution was amorphous; the atrocities were represented as generalised facets of Nazi criminality, rather than any specific focus on the Jews.

[118] Much material is covered in Robert Abzug, *Inside the Vicious Heart: Americans and the Liberation of Nazi Concentration Camps* (New York: Oxford University Press, 1985). See 118.

[119] Roger Lanze, "The German Prisons and Concentration Camps," 26 May 1945, Memorandum in Folder "Captured Agents," 7th Army, Box #246, File Series, Entry 210, OSS Classified Sources and Methods File, RG 226, Records of the OSS, 1940-46, NARA, CP, MD.

[120] This is not to say that, as Tony Kushner has pointed out, the liberation scenes were not minimised of their "Jewishness": *The Holocaust and the Liberation Imagination* (Oxford: Oxford University Press, 1994). Furthermore, Abzug found that some GIs were desperate to forget what they had seen: *Inside the Vicious Heart*, 118.

keen to describe the gruesome spectacle for American audiences. "I made the visit [to Buchenwald] deliberately, in order to be in a position to give first-hand evidence of these things if ever, in the future, there develops a tendency to charge these allegations merely to 'propaganda.'"[121] General Hobart Gay, accompanying a grouchy General Patton to the camp, made a similar point: "It is a shame not more people cannot see such things, particularly the politicians, who, after all, bring on wars".[122] Patton himself, according to an account by General Eisenhower, "would not even enter" a particular room in Buchenwald. "He said he would get sick if he did so."[123]

Images of the charnel houses and the emaciated bodies proved defining features in initial reactions to German atrocities. They placed the victim of the Final Solution at the forefront of American political perception while highlighting the more sinister aspects of the executioners. Buchenwald was described by the *New York Times* as "a factory of death for political and military prisoners."[124] Other writers also added their observations to the inventory of horror. Journalist Martha Gellhorn was characteristically grim and vivid in her description of what she saw at Dachau. "Behind the barbed wire and the electric fence, the skeletons sat in the sun and searched themselves for lice."[125] The account by a captain of XX Corps to his wife was particularly shocked at the two main SS commanders at Ohrdruf who would pass the time by sitting and watching "the burning of the weeks accumulation of dead while they joked and drank whiskey."[126]

Faith in the Germans as human beings was low, diminished by the grotesque revelations of the newly liberated landscape. The American prisoners of war on Gellhorn's C-47 flight in May 1945 were adamant that they "never wanted to see Germany again."[127] The Germans were only fit as subjects for severe punishment, re-education and de-nazification. In 1944, an interesting report from a U.S. officer on Allied discussions about how indoctrination procedures would be implemented after the war discussed the use of certain "literature," thereby revealing a somewhat crude view of the authoritarian executioner. The German was a complete ignoramus, morally

---

[121] Eisenhower to Marshall, Letter dated April 15, 1945, noted in Blumenson, ed., *Patton Papers*, 688.

[122] April 15, 1945, recorded in Blumenthal, ed., *Patton Papers*, 687.

[123] Eisenhower, Letter to Marshall, April 15, 1945 cited in *The Patton Papers*, 688.

[124] "Buchenwald," *New York Times*, April 19, 1945, C26.

[125] Martha Gellhorn, *The Face of War* (London: Virago Press, 1986), 172.

[126] Alois J. Leitnen (Ohrdruf), XX Corps, G-Section, to Gretchen, Appleton, WI, April 13, 1945, the document available at www.uwm.edu/Library/arch/holocaust/lietnen.htm, accessed May 23, 2004.

[127] Gellhorn, *The Face of War*, 172.

naive and easily trainable for Allied purposes. The German prisoner of war is treated as something like an obedient guinea pig. "Use of as many U.S. Newspapers and Magazines, N.Y. Times, Life, Time, etc. [to indoctrinate the captives] but not a paper in German especially for the prisoner." Showing the depth of reading by the officers behind this policy, the only German books to be provided were to be "by well known German liberal thinkers such as Thomas Mann".[128]

In April 1945, American forces took residents of Weimar for a "tour" of the Buchenwald camp, a forced pedagogic exercise that planted images of the Final Solution in the minds of residents who had claimed to be unsuspecting of the atrocities. The exercise was as much a lesson for the locals as it was for the U.S. soldiers present. "I have written [the piece on Buchenwald]," wrote Lt. Colonel Charles R. Codman, senior aide to General Patton, "because I thought I ought to."[129] The evidence was ghastly, even unbelievable. "*Au fond* I don't like horrors any more than you do," he explained in the attached letter to the editor. "It probably won't be believed – even with the dozens of photographs I had taken."[130] Believability, even for the author, was difficult: "Barrack 47" was beyond him, its stench, its nightmare: he "frankly ... hadn't the stomach for it."[131]

As for Patton, he "was so deeply moved by this thing [Buchenwald] that I had the leading citizens of Weimar, to the extent of some 1,500, marched through the camp and made to look at the horrid spectacle".[132] In the words of one of Patton's letters, "We have lately been liberating the slave camps, and honestly, words are inadequate to express the horror of those institutions."[133] The Mayor of Ohrdruf, who had seen the sight previously, expressed shock: "I had no idea this was going on in my municipality." His reaction was to join the victims through suicide. One of Patton's soldiers regarded this as noble. "I think the Mayor of Ohrdruf was just one of those oversensitive Germans. No good to the Reich. Better out of the way."[134] The morally confused German is

[128] C. Skilbeck, Lt. Colonel, PID Liaison, Ottowa, "Report on Liaison Visit to Special Projects Division Office of the Provost Marshal General, U.S. Army, Dec 1944," Secret. Folder: Post Hostilities Use of Prisoners, Box #291, Entry 210, OSS Classified Resources and Methods File; Records of the OSS, 1940-46, RG 226, NARA, CP, MD.

[129] Charles E. Codman, "For the Record: Buchenwald," *The Atlantic Monthly* 176 (July 1945): 54-6, 54.

[130] Codman, "Buchenwald," 54.

[131] Codman, "Buchenwald," 55.

[132] Letter from Patton to Marshall, enclosed with photos, date not mentioned (probably between April 21 and 27, 1941), in Blumenson, ed., *Patton Papers*, 692.

[133] GSP, Jr., to Scott, April 15, 1945, Blumenson, ed., *The Patton Papers*, 686.

[134] Codman, "Buchenwald," 56.

a recurring trope in the initial observations of the Final Solution. In the accounts that fill the periodicals of the time, there is little clue that U.S. foreign policy would in time redeem Germany, cleansing it of its record with financial favours and military dispensations.

EXPEDITIOUS POLICIES, 1945-1949

The initial shock of U.S. leaders and military representatives as the camps were liberated realized the victims of the Third Reich as beings with historical potency: their legacy was to be preserved, their fate to be remembered. But this view of German atrocities proved provisional. Such a viewing of the as yet unnamed Holocaust was based on an immediate desire to ameliorate the condition of the survivors. In time, the victims immortalised in Eisenhower's rhetoric as beings to be never forgotten, begin losing their relevance. The authorities empathise with the convicts as future warriors against Bolshevism; the convict is not so fundamentally evil (a conventional Holocaust theme) that he cannot be inserted back into society for the sake of progress.

Foremost in the minds of the occupation forces was imparting the benefits of an expeditious war crimes policy, rapid in trial and execution of sentences. As Jackson had recommended to President Harry S. Truman in his report on Nuremberg, the theatre of another large-scale tribunal, or a series of "second international trials", was undesirable.[135] In a message to Brigadier General George F. Schulgen of the Civil Affairs Division of the War Department, the U.S. governor for Germany Lucius Clay was found to be "apprehensive [...] that second trials will result in emphasizing ideological differences which could defeat purpose." Agreement for Jackson's suggestion for zonal trials "under agreed policies have some advantages."[136] Legal theatre was to be kept to a minimum, in a manner that was inconceivable fifteen years later at the Eichmann Trial where the courtroom became the scene of didactic scolding by the state of Israel. As Clay himself urged in a despatch in early September 1946, trials in the U.S. zone of occupation were to be quick: "it is important that there be no delay between passing of sentence at Nuremberg and the start of the trials in the U.S. zone." Openly, Clay noted how "our policies in

[135] See for instance, Robert H. Jackson, *Final Report to the Secretary of the Army on the Nuremberg War Crimes Trials Under Control Council Law No. 10* (Washington, D.C: United States Government Printer, 1950), 22-27.

[136] Clay Personal for Schulgen, 4 August 1946, CC 1206 Secret, in Jean Edward Smith, ed., *The Papers of General Lucius Clay* (Bloomington, Ind.: Indiana University Press, 1974), I, 247.

Germany require that the punishment administered as a result of trial in United States courts be executed quickly and certainly."[137]

A date for completion was tentatively advanced: December 1947. But in 1948, the trials were still going, and Clay "tried to expedite the trials and set July 1, 1948, as the target date for completion," a hope that would not be realized till April 1949. Americans at home were getting weary, and the Department of the Army was stirring for their termination.[138] Clay's chief reviewing role of the Dachau convictions was significant: 1672 individuals had been judged and 256 acquitted. According to his account: "I set aside 69 convictions, commuted 119 sentences, and reduced 138, leaving 1090 sentences; 426 of the convictions carried the death sentence."[139]

In May 1948, we find Clay's interest in the welfare of Germany's war criminals and their influence over the overall political situation undiminished. Initially, Clay noted the growing number of convicts on death row, and how this would be potentially explosive for the justice-conscious American people. "As a result of delays in review, stay of sentence pending possible appeal to the Supreme Court, et cetera, the death sentences imposed by military courts on Germans charged with the murder of concentration camp inmates, prisoners of war, et cetera, has accumulated until there is now in excess of five hundred awaiting execution." Despite seemingly proper procedures behind obtaining these sentences, Clay found "it difficult to adjust [his] own mental processes to requiring what looks to be almost a mass execution of more than five hundred persons." Carrying out the executions would give "an appearance of cruelty to the United States even though there is no question in my mind that the crimes committed fully justify the death penalty." [140]

The pressure on Clay was particularly acute at this time. Indeed, four days earlier, Clay had fended off a pointed attack by German clerics spearheaded by Bishop Wurm with a letter claiming that such a campaign of criticism on Allied war crimes policy was aimed at discrediting "a court which with high intent is endeavouring to establish precedents in international law which may serve to prevent the world being plunged into chaos."[141] But the tilt in favour of leniency was beginning. Six days after responding to Wurm, Clay requested

[137] From Clay Personal for ECHOLS, CC 3057 Confidential, 4 September 1946, in *Clay Papers*, I, 261-2, 262.

[138] Lucius D. Clay, *Decision in Germany* (Melbourne: Heinemann, 1950), 252.

[139] Clay, *Decision in Germany*, 253.

[140] Clay for Draper, CC 4433, Top Secret-Eyes Only, 24 May 1948, in *Clay Papers*, II, 658.

[141] Clay to Wurm, 19 June 1948, IfZ, MF 260, OMGUS-Akten, AG 1949/75/3 (Archiv des Instituts für Zeitgeschichte), München [Archives of the Institute for Modern History, Munich], noted in Frei, *Adenauer's Germany*, 107.

the formation of clemency boards to alleviate the potential spectre of mass execution. The currency of lenient disposition could not be seen to be in short supply.

"Believe clemency board badly needed and would appreciate its immediate selection. Problem is urgent and final action on sentences is necessary as soon as possible. Hence, I would urge selection of members who can become immediately available."[142]

Adding to this onset of leniency towards the German war convicts was the notion that the German soldier had been a victim of overzealous U.S. prosecutors and soldiers.[143] Enraged American soldiers were accused of standing by in some cases, allowing German SS troops to be beaten to death by liberated inmates. In some instances, they even joined in. "Few Americans found it hard to hate the Germans after encountering survivors of their premeditated bestiality".[144]

Dachau bore witness to such slaughter in April 1945, an episode that was promptly investigated by the U.S. Seventh Army. In the testimony of Major Carl F. Woost, taken at Dachau, "with no training in investigations of this sort it would be extremely difficult [to determine the extent of the responsibility of American soldiers]."[145] William L. Competielle testified that, "The word just got around that they were going to shoot all the SS'rs."[146] How naive it was, argued one commentator, "to expect men who were risking their lives every day to be scrupulous at all times in the observance of the rights of private property of the enemy."[147]

Bursts of savagery against concentration camp guards were also accompanied by publicity occasioned by the rough tactics employed by overzealous interrogators. Journals throughout the late 1940s noted that German convicts had been treated with extreme brutality by their American counterparts. In the words of a *Commentary* contributing editor, these reports noted how "a number of Germans convicted of war crimes had been subjected

[142] Clay [in London] Personal and Eyes Only for Draper, 73372 Top Secret, 26 May 1948, in *Clay Papers*, II, 659.

[143] There was also the case against the Nuremberg trial itself and whether any valid prosecution could have been made in the first place. The debates are summarized in various works, most notably in Bosch, *Judgment on Nuremberg*.

[144] Engler, "The Individual Soldier," 82.

[145] A. White, Major General, G.S.C, Chief of Staff, Memorandum to Inspector General, Seventh Army, Office of the Chief of Staff, APO TSS, c/o Postmaster New York, 21 May, 1945, 1-120, 7 (herein *Seventh Army investigation*).

[146] Testimony taken in May 4, 1945, at Pullach, by Lt. Col. Joseph M. Whitaker, Assistant Inspector General, Seventh Army, in *Seventh Army Investigation*, 18.

[147] Engler, "The Individual Soldier," 82.

to atrocious brutalities by American investigators."[148] Perpetrators of war crimes became victims, their rights trampled on. Inquiries were demanded and made. The fuss created over allegations made by those behind the Malmédy murders, where U.S. prisoners had been summarily executed by an SS outfit led by SS officer Joachim Peiper, raised considerable publicity at home.

Even if the Malmédy massacres had occurred against American soldiers as opposed to Jewish victims, the controversy had the effect of tarnishing the legal response to Germany's atrocities. In March 1949, the *New York Times* published comments from the Administration of Justice Review Board which found, in the paper's words, "irregularities in the treatment of the accused, including physical force and threats that if they did not talk, their relatives would lose their ration cards."[149] The Board, charged with investigating the allegations behind the interrogations of the Malmédy executioners received a petition from Willis M. Everett Jr., alleging the use of "mock trials" designed to "soften up" the suspects. These trials, so the petition discussed, were somewhat idiosyncratic: the prisoner would be hooded and brought into a dark room illuminated by a candle on a table, decked by covers and a crucifix. U.S. officers impersonating judges would then proceed to interrogate.[150]

Alarmed at the prospect of any possible commuting of the death-sentences, the Society for the Prevention of World War III, headed by its active President Mark van Doren, cabled Clay from its headquarters in Madison Avenue, urging the immediate carrying out of the sentences. Other U.S. officers argued that there had been no miscarriage of justice. Major Dwight Fanton, investigator into the Malmédy cases, rejected charges of brutality. Morris Elowitz, Assistant Trial Judge Advocate claimed that all "confessions were voluntary", and treatment had been humane, evidence of which lay in a decent supply of tobacco rations for the prisoners.[151] Clay noted that: "Members of the prosecution staff testified to the use of stage settings, stool pigeons, and similar measures to extract evidence." This was the verdict of Clay's own Administration of Justice Review Board and the Simpson Commission that had been set up by the Department of the Army. However, the more serious charges "were denied by the prosecution staff and not borne out by other evidence."[152] Clay sympathised with the American soldier.

[148] Nathan Glazer, "The Method of Senator McCarthy: Its Origins, Its Uses, Its Prospects," *Commentary* 15 (1953): 244-56, 244.

[149] *New York Times*, "US Board Critical of Malmedy Case," March 5, 1949, 1, 4, col. 2.

[150] *New York Times*, "US Board Critical," 4.

[151] *New York Times*, "Two US Investigators Disavow Abuse of Germans at Malmedy," March 5, 1949, 4, col. 2.

[152] Clay, *Decision in Germany*, 253.

"While any use of improper methods was to be deplored, the Army had been shocked beyond measure at the cold blooded murder of our soldiers at Malmédy."[153]

These notes on the Malmédy investigations were significant, since they deflated American confidence in the veracity of some verdicts, however reliable they may have been on the whole. The basis of Nuremberg, including the more severe convictions based on the crimes of the Holocaust, was potentially discredited in the broader political discussion which tended to favour the convicts. While it might be assumed that the American administrators might have shown a preference for harsh punishment towards Germans accused of committing atrocities against their soldiers (in preference say to those committed against Jews), the converse was true in some circles. Executioner "welfare" proved to be the overarching requirement of good governance, a feature that tended to gloss over the juridically exceptional category of "crimes against humanity".

Indeed, the Senate subcommittee established under the stewardship of Senator Raymond Baldwin to investigate the case had to contend with an indignant Senator Joseph Macarthy, who resigned after a mere four weeks citing reluctance on the part of members to make findings negative to American soldiers.[154] Clay observed with some irritation as a reviewer of the Dachau trials that the Malmédy accusations would "cast some discredit on those trials as a whole" specifically those cases dealing with German "participation in the murders and cruelties of the concentration camps, in the murder of our airmen, who were forced to parachute to supposed safety within Germany, and the murder of unarmed, surrendered American soldiers."[155] The Baldwin subcommittee concurred, arguing that the "mock trials so prejudiced the thinking of all who reviewed this case that they resulted in otherwise guilty men escaping the death sentence or perhaps going entirely free."[156]

There were also various obstacles that presented themselves to the U.S. occupation authorities in dealing with the perpetrators: practical difficulties in obtaining trial, the concerns with the American public that justice had to be seen to be done. The American desire to reform the German civil service was evident in Control Law Eight, which ultimately subjected the civil service to ideological surgery, but the mechanism for blanket punishments did not

[153] Clay, *Decision in Germany*, 253.
[154] Frei, *Adenauer's Germany*, 117.
[155] Clay, *Decision in Germany*, 252-3.
[156] U.S. Senate Committee on Armed Services, Subcommittee, Malmédy Massacre Investigation, 81st Cong., 1st sess., 1949 (the Baldwin Report), 31.

exist.[157] The jurist Herbert Wechsler suggested that two million or so suspects could have easily been tried but for "inescapable ambiguities in the measure of their actual scope [of guilt]." Trials lasting years were in the offing, and the officialdom of occupied Germany had no desire to compromise political expediency for scrupulous legal procedures.[158]

The lure of pragmatism demanded a flexible bending of principles. While the CROWCASS list involved a compilation of mass criminality, it "did not imply the ability to bring them to trial."[159] What in fact transpired were delays in trial that "solidified" German support for the "poor, persecuted Nazis".[160] The focus here seemed to be less on the severity of the crimes than the modification of their punishment. The banker, the scientist and some bureaucrats were dispensed from the regime of "universal" punishment. A Senate subcommittee heard evidence from a denazification board of appeal of the United States Forces European Theatre that keeping an important Nazi industrialist free and active was entirely justified on the basis of American values of "private property". Since National Socialism constituted a "social revolution" for Germany, the appropriation of property from industrialists was "not in conformity with American standards [in dealing with private property]." The reasoning of the committee was revealing. The image of German capital and industrial might, singled out in the Nuremberg indictments as causative of totalitarian crimes, was banished. A member of the Political division saw this industrialist as "extremely capable", "a kind of Henry Ford."[161]

Even Jackson, whose emphasis on legal universalism was unqualified in his legal performance at Nuremberg, feared subjecting industrialists (many of whom had used slave labour) to trial. Such action might "discourage industrial co-operation with our Government in maintaining its defences in the future while not at all weakening the Soviet position, since they [did] not rely upon

---

157 Doman, "Political Consequences," 87.

158 See Herbert Wechsler, "The Issues of the Nuremberg Trial," *Political Science Quarterly* 62 (March 1947): 11-26, 21-2.

159 Earl F. Ziemke, *The U.S. Army in the Occupation of Germany, 1944-1946* (Washington: Centre of Military History, United States Army, 1975), 392. The suspect list ultimately reached 150,000. For a contrary view, see Doman, who claimed there was nothing "fantastic in the prosecution of a few million persons": "Political Consequences," 87.

160 Karl Heinrich Knappstein, "Die versäumte Revolution," *Die Wandlung*, Jg. 2, Heft 8 (November, 1947): 663-77, 748, noted in William E. Griffith, "Denazification in the United States Zone of Germany," *Annals of the American Academy of Political and Social Science* 267 (January 1950): 68-76, 72.

161 *Elimination of German Resources for War*, 79th Congress, 1st sess., Hearings before a Subcommittee of the Committee on Military Affairs, Senate, February 23, 1946, part 11, 1545, noted in Engler, "The Individual Soldier," 79.

private enterprise".[162] The process of leniency was so advanced that the American counsel prosecuting the chemical firm I. G. Farben saw fit to comment. Finding the ideological conditions of the Cold War gradually erode the precedent of Nuremberg, he felt that in "treating such groups as friends, we are losing true friends all over the world."[163]

The regime of uneven justice in American policies on German war crimes and crimes against humanity, were revealed in areas of American administration, the local Stadtkreis being a specific example of this. John Gimbel's micro-study of Marburg denazification revealed that the clemency regime was well extended into the Stadtkreis by 1946. In July 1946, OMGUS amended the "Law for Liberation". These measures proved significant in narrowing the scope for punishing offences: those born after January 1, 1919 were exempted under the Youth amnesty; unless they fell into various major criminal categories, while the Christmas amnesty of 1946 targeted low-income groups and cripples (those more than 50 percent disabled), again depending on the nature of the crimes.[164] Clay himself observed in his memoirs on the first years of U.S. occupation how prosecution proved difficult in numerous instances. His response to criticism at the release of "a Schacht who had been kept in prison under the law for three years, and letting a Von Papen off with exclusion from office and a heavy fine" was one of practical consideration. Even at Nuremberg, officials had found it difficult to implicate Nazi officials in "the conspiracy to wage aggressive war".[165] Furthermore, a Howard University academic found, after perusing the case law on various trials in the American zone of occupied Germany, numerous cases of leniency. Evidence cited included an "amnestied" defendant who "subsequently [spat] on the face of a victim of Nazism and expressed her regret that not all concentration camp inmates had been killed." Another notable case was a German doctor who was fined the sum of 500 marks for "the execution of the sterilization law".[166]

One prime representative of "Fordist" capitalism, unburdened by any reflection on the Holocaust, was the influential industrialist Alfred Krupp von

---

[162] Memo for President [Truman] from Jackson, May 13, 1946, quoted in Bloxham, "The Trial That Never Was," 51.

[163] Josiah E. Dubois, Jr., *The Devil's Chemists: 24 Conspirators of the Institute Farben Cartel Who Manufactured War*s (Boston, 1952), x, 338-56; noted in Marck E. Spicka, "The Devil's Chemists on Trial: The American Prosecution of I.G. Farben at Nuremberg," *The Historian* 61, 4 (1999): 865-882.

[164] John Gimbel, "American Denazification and German Local Politics, 1945-1949: A Case Study in Marburg," *American Political Science Review* 54, 1 (March, 1960): 83-105, 96-7.

[165] Clay, *Decision in Germany*, 261.

[166] *Frankfurter Rundschau*, April 29, 1948, *Mittelbayrische Zeitung* (Regensburg), June 18, 1948, cited by Herz, "Fiasco of Denazification," 587, 585.

Bohlen, imprisoned for twelve years and seeking clemency in 1950 under the more conciliatory eyes of Germany's U.S. Commissioner John J. McCloy. His Krupp firm had been accused of using slave labour, and he himself convicted for various charges he regarded as "novel" and inappropriate for an "economist". Over the charges that he had used concentration camp inmates, working them to the point of exhaustion and death, his excuse, explained in his petition for release, was plain: they were not of his own doing. He was, so went the submission, a good capitalist, with a reputable firm that was trying to make ends meet in a totalitarian state. Merely using slavery did not mean "approval of the concentration camp idea"; and the firm had done all it could to ameliorate the poor diet of the workers.[167]

In time, some American papers noted that the U.S. occupation policy had been less than satisfactory in prosecuting those responsible for their assortment of crimes and atrocities. The uneven nature of Nuremberg justice was picked up by the *Chicago Tribune* in February, 1947. "The moral degradation of the Army of Occupation in Germany has advanced so far that all sense of distinction between honourable and dishonourable conduct has been lost.... The standards of American justice have been degraded. The pretense that the full historical record [of German crimes] was to be exposed was fraudulent from the start".[168] Clay fired off an indignant cable, finding the article "vicious and slanderous," engendering enough animosity on his part to prepare a "possible suit in the in the name of the Army of Occupation and its members."[169] But the process of such "degradation" had merely begun, symptomatic of the Final Solution as a phenomenon in the 1950s of convict-welfare rather than the collective memory of the slain.

Clemency and Exoneration

In 1978, John J. McCloy was given the Aspen Institute Statesman Humanist Award. Various individuals who had had dealings with the first head of the World Bank, and second High Commissioner for Germany, emphasised various qualities. In rehabilitating Germany, he had always been guided by

---

[167] Krupp to Lucius D. Clay, 21 August 1948, Nuernberg Prison, Petition, in Krupp, Alfried, Case no. 10 Folder, #1 Petitions, Box #16 in NARA, RG 466, Office of the United States High Commissioner for Germany, Records of Persons Convicted by the US Military Tribunals at Nuremberg, Prisons Division, 1945-57.

[168] *Chicago Tribune*, February 28, 1947.

[169] Clay Personal for Draper CC 3379, Confidential, 3 March 1948, in *Clay Papers*, II, 565.

law as "organised freedom and equality" and bringer of peace. He was also considered a fair man always capable of putting "the general interest above his personal interest".[170] The entire clemency fever in American policy towards occupied Germany was taken to new steps during the years of U.S. High Commissioner McCloy, whose vision of Germany depended less on punitive measures than those of healing a nation in moral convalescence. McCloy exuded the mantras of "the free world" in opposition to the world "enslaved". He found Alexis de Tocqueville prophetic and instructive, when he wrote that "there are two colossi in the world: the one, as Tocqueville said, free, and the other slave." The criminality of his concern did not reside in American-controlled prisons in Germany, but behind the Iron Curtain, where the Soviets chose to wage a policy based on "aggressive war or the gallows."[171]

His view of the atrocities committed by the German war criminals held at Landsberg and under the jurisdiction of the U.S. Army, including those accused of crimes against humanity, was less preoccupied with avenging victims than focusing on executioner welfare. The criminal characteristics of the prisoners were subordinated to broader issues of welfare, justice and the politics of German integration into a European Defense Community, with strong Franco-German support.[172] Such an interest was shared by Washington, in line with the historical events of 1949-1950 that involved a France weakened by its Indochina War, the Soviet acquisition of atomic weaponry, the Truman administration's desire to reduce budget outlays, and the outbreak of the Korean War.[173]

The Federal Republic would become part of a united Europe that would constitute a "skeleton key" to the various challenges posed by the Soviets, the Franco-German association, and economic and political issues.[174] As the *Atlantic* editorialised in the fall of 1953, "Since the Bonn government of West Germany came into being four years ago, a fundamental aim of American policy has been to Europeanize Germany." By this, the policy was meant to force Germany "westward", a vision that had "been one of Dulles's most cherished dreams." Underpinning this rationale was the need to pool "German

[170] Comments from respectively Willy Brandt, Averell Harriman and Eric Severeid, in J. J. McCloy, *In the Public Service – On Receipt of the Aspen Institute Statesman Humanist Award* (New York: Aspen Institute of Humanistic Studies, 1978), 15, 20, 23.

[171] John J. McCloy, *The Challenge to American Foreign Policy* (Cambridge, MA: Harvard University Press, 1953), 2-3.

[172] See particular Thomas A. Schwartz, "The 'Skeleton-Key' - European Foreign Policy, European Unity, and German Rearmament, 1949-54," *Central European History* 19, 4 (December 1986): 369-85.

[173] Schwartz, "The 'Skeleton-Key,'" 372.

[174] Schwartz, "The 'Skeleton-Key,'" 380-1.

manpower" to readily defend Western Europe and "that only through absorption of Germany into Europe can the danger of German national military power be avoided."[175]

In 1950, the ambitious Chancellor Konrad Adenauer pleaded with McCloy to be generous towards the war criminals. This was only natural, explained the German Chancellor in December, as many Germans "considered the verdicts to be exceedingly harsh." Leaving aside the fact that some of the Landsberg criminals had been responsible for crimes against humanity, Adenauer lessened their culpability. "This feeling [of resentment from large parts of the German population] is the more understandable as all the defendants were acquitted of the charges of crimes against the peace and of conspiracy to commit such crimes." Pursuant to consultation with the chairman of the Clemency Board, it was desirable for the Commissioner to "grant clemency on a generous scale."[176]

In 1951, war criminals who had been sentenced as a result of trials in the U.S. zone (such figures as those involved in the Einzatzgruppen) submitted their cases for lesser sentences to McCloy. The results were mixed: the sentences of such individuals as Otto Ohlendorf were reaffirmed. But the war criminals at Landsberg who were not reprieved had become the subject of a political game. Those who did not follow their executed comrades to the gallows had their sentences reduced, exposing a certain arbitrariness that did not go unnoticed.

The Cold War atmosphere was beginning to take effect. The submissions downplaying the significance of some who had participated in the Holocaust, arguing that the true perpetrators of crimes – the other holocaust – lay in the East behind the impenetrable Iron Curtain.

Victim politics proved remarkably fluid, beings switched from victims of Nazism to victims of Communism. The correspondence with the U.S. authorities during this period is notable for its Cold War highlights, stressing the use of Communist crimes in distinction to Nazi atrocities. A letter to Clay from a concerned German writer, Dorothee T. L. Schiffer, in October 1948 contained poetry for Krupp's release.

"And save Germany, Again and again the rumour can be heard, that a threatening wave from the east would come over us and destroy everything up to the channel before you have a chance to get your ships over. My child, my

---

175 Editorial, "Is Germany Unity good for Europe?" *The Atlantic* 192 (September, 1953): 6. The reference is to Eisenhower's Secretary of State John Foster Dulles.

176 Adenauer to John J. McCloy, US trans. Z991/50, 5 December 1950, in Folder 321.6, Krupp, Alfred, HICOG, Petitions, Box 16, RG 466, NARA, CP, MD.

daughter, is among them."[177] On his release, a Krupp admirer with previous contacts with the firm in Australia, and member of the Australian-American association, found the verdict a well-fashioned weapon against the Eastern Bloc. "In these times when the union of all anti-Communistic countries is of such vital importance for the future well-being of the world, your courageous action deserved to be valued as a powerful contribution to paving the way towards a better understanding between those nations who must combine in the interests of peace."[178]

The correspondence with McCloy on Krupp by observers, including Krupp admirers and employees, revealed the significant pressure, and gratitude, to show leniency to the industrialist as the compassionate employer, and even the victim of totalitarian authority.

Krupp the criminal metamorphosed dramatically into Krupp as a paragon of democratic virtue, his release occasioned, not by political calculation but by respect for "independent" judicial processes.

McCloy in effect makes Krupp's release a showcase of American justice, an example to those behind the Iron Curtain familiar with show trials based on flimsy evidence. From Athens, representatives of the Krupp firm found his release commendable.

"We believe that, under the condition of the present time, the granting of justice, not being influenced by political considerations, constitutes the best, as for the removal, among peoples, of the mistrust and enmities created by the war."[179] From Santiago, it was noted that "public opinion in Chile took special notice of this fact [of Krupp's 'liberation']".[180]

The wording from Turkish employees was even more grandiose, labelling the decision as one "appreciated by the entire civilized world and will demonstrate once more that justice is free from all political influences in democratic countries."[181]

---

177 Schiffer to Lucius C. Clay, 30 October 1948, trans. 19 November 1948, in Folder Krupp, Alfried, Case No. 10, Folder #1, Petitions, Box #16, Petitions for Clemency, HICOG, RG 466, NARA, CP, MD.

178 A. Hoette to McCloy, For the Attention of the High Commissioner, from Melbourne, 27 March 1951, Folder 321.6-Krupp, Alfred, Box #16, Petitions, HICOG, RG 466, NARA, CP, MD.

179 Société Générale de Machines, "G. Castritis & Cie S.A." to Mr. McCloy, Athens, March 19, 1951, Folder 321.6 Krupp, Box #16, Petitions for Clemency, HICOG, RG 466, NARA, CP, MD.

180 E. Schuchard to McCloy, High Commissioner for Germany, Santiago, 22 March 1951, Folder 321.6 – Krupp, Alfred Box #16, Petitions, HICOG, RG 466, NARA, CP, MD.

181 Süha Fazli Taylan to John McClay [sic], Istanbul, 19 March 1951, in Folder 321.6-Krupp, Alfred Folder, Box #16, Petitions, HICOG, RG 466, NARA, CP, MD.

The reaction at home to McCloy's decisions was not entirely glowing. The High Commissioner had to reassure the editor of *Der Aufbau*, a German Jewish paper in New York, that his policies did not constitute a "general amnesty" for all German war criminals.[182] A community group calling itself the Women's Council for Peace was outraged by the generous decisions, as expressed in a letter by one of its members, Mildred Gleit. "We feel a deep, burning anger and humiliation at the recent decision of the American government of West Germany to grant clemency to 89 Nazi War criminals." The anger was two-pronged, and resonant with the politics of atrocity victims. The organisation was aggrieved that the American occupation force could have been so callous as to "grant clemency to the murderers of 142 unarmed American prisoners of war at Malmedy [sic], Belgium, during the Battle of the Bulge in 1944." It was shocked that America's "consciences" had succumbed to an amnesiac fit in forgetting "the slave labor camps – the gas chambers – the mass annihilation of millions of Jews, Catholics and Protestants at the hands of these men". Krupp received particularly harsh treatment as the man "who financed Hitler," a money venture that led to "the death of our sons, husbands and relatives." Gleit's final call was against forgetting and placing the victim at the forefront of political considerations in dealing with a defeated Germany. "We say our consciences will not allow us to forget the past – and let bygones be bygones!"[183]

In Congress, Senator Jacob Javits expressed worries that America's moral standing had been affected by the Landsberg decisions.[184] His doubts had already developed by late 1948, when he formed the opinion that U.S. occupation policy had "appeared to me to be too soft on the former Nazis."[185] He proposed a Congressional inquiry into the wisdom of U.S. occupation policy, the findings of which were, in his words, ultimately "buried". Nor could Javits accept the notion that a new Germany could act as a "bulwark" or "buffer" state against the East.[186]

McCloy was displeased. The war criminals were the untouchable issue. Policy towards their welfare was an American interest that would be damaged

[182] McCloy to *Der Aufbau* Chief Editor Manfred George, in *Neue Zeitung*, September 5 1950, in Frei, *Adenauer's Germany*, 150.

[183] Mildred Gleit, Women's Council for Peace, Marmion Av., New York, to McCloy, February 2, 1951, in Folder 321.6, Krupp, Alfred, Box #16, Petitions, HICOG, RG 466, NARA, CP, MD.

[184] See *Congressional Record*, May 10, 1951, A 2812.

[185] Jacob K. Javits, *Javits: An Autobiography of a Public Man* (Boston: Houghton & Mifflin Co., 1981), 186.

[186] Javits, *Javits*, 186.

by overly enthusiastic humanitarians at home. "As I have said before," he responded in a reproachful reply to Javits, "it is of greatest importance in Germany and Europe today that the United States avoid giving the impression of disagreement and lack of clarity about its foreign policy – and this, I believe, would be the inevitable effect of the investigation you propose." He conceded that "changes in policy" had occurred towards occupied Germany, though reiterating the familiar platform that "the extirpation of Nazism and the fostering of democracy" remained key aims of the Administration.[187] To abridge these themes in favour of "more expedient aims, would be criminally negligent and dangerous."[188]

McCloy continued to discuss the relevant features of war crimes politics, which highlighted the rights of the defendant, rather than the severity of the crimes. It was because of "a fundamental principle of American justice that persons accused shall have the right of appeal." He dismissed any suggestions that German participation in the new defence arrangements had been bought, as the Clemency Board submitted its report on August 1950, "a month before the matter of German participation was first raised at the New York Conference of Foreign Ministers." As for the burning issue – the release of Krupp – McCloy could see no reason in keeping a mere "junior" of the firm in prison whose role in "the use of slave labour" was "very doubtful," and more "the effect of a notorious name." The symbolic resonance of war crimes and the Final Solution held no practical significance for McCloy: "I was not concerned with a symbol [of Krupp as evil]." In conclusion, the Landsberg decisions, far from revealing a growing laxity in U.S. policies towards the punishment of atrocities, had revealed the "true nature of the Nazi crimes" to the German public.[189] To such figures of public standing as Eleanor Roosevelt, who were critical of the policy, McCloy's arguments promoted a type of German war criminal with American-styled rights of review. The review board was necessary to add some equivalent review body present in England or the United States: "[U]nlike criminal cases in the U.S. and England there was no provision for further court review of these cases for possible errors of law or fact after the court of first instance had passed them."[190]

---

[187] High Commissioner McCloy to J. K. Javits, "The Present Order of German Government," in *Department of State Bulletin* 24 (June 11, 1951): 940-2, 941.

[188] McCloy to Javits, "The Present Order," 941.

[189] McCloy to Javits, "The Present Order," 941-2.

[190] McCloy to Eleanor Roosevelt, March 12, 1951, folder J. J. McCloy, Eleanor Roosevelt Papers, Box 3913, Franklin D. Roosevelt Library; noted in Thomas A. Schwartz, *America's Germany: John J. McCloy and the Federal Republic of Germany* (Cambridge, MA: Harvard University Press, 1991), 172.

McCloy's humbling suggestions that neither political expediency nor the familiar horse-trading over the issue of German participation in Europe's defense was taking place, does not stand up to scrutiny. Officially, McCloy's report on Germany in 1952 was the prognosis of a satisfied doctor on a well-performed patient. All the better, went the tone of the report, given the presence of other viruses in the vicinity. Germany had become a "peaceful member of the European community ... desirous of resisting the communist threat."[191] The diplomatic correspondence later that year reveals a keen Adenauer, less interested in honouring dead Jews than in consolidating the position of a divided Germany.

The perpetrators of the Holocaust become the political capital of U.S.-West German manoeuvring, assimilated into a general category of war criminals. A telegram from acting High Commissioner for Germany Reber in December 1952 found Adenauer worried to make political gains on the release of war criminals, so much so he demanded the resolution of the problem before the entry of Germany into any security arrangements. "It would be of great importance if some announcement would be made by allies during current Paris mtg [sic] indicating their intentions immediately to make far reaching gesture towards solution of war-criminals problem."[192] Britain, the Chancellor was keen to point out, had been far more lenient than their American allies on the issue.

Timing was everything, as the issue would "affect the formation of German units for the European Defense Community, since these units would be composed in large measure of technicians and specialists who would be difficult to recruit unless there was a more lenient parole system for the war criminals."[193]

Adenauer was not content to keep the matter in McCloy's hands. He even pressured President Dwight D. Eisenhower for a decision on the subject. As keen as the President was on resolving the issue – a sentiment he expressed in a meeting with Adenauer's personal representative Blankenhorn in the summer of 1953, he had to be frank that any such move might displease the French – an outcome that would be against the interests of Washington and Bonn. "What he [Eisenhower] had in mind was that the reaction in France

---

[191] *Department of State Bulletin*, "US High Commissioner McCloy Submits his Final Report on Germany," Letter dated July 31, 1952, 27 (December 8, 1952): 903-7.

[192] Acting US High Commissioner for Germany (Reber) to Department of State, Telegram 762A.00/12-1652, Bonn, December 16, 1952, in *FRUS*, 1952-4, VII, 392-3.

[193] U.S. Delegate Minutes of the First General Meeting of Chancellor Adenauer and Secretary Dulles, Conference Suite, 1778, Pennsylvania Avenue, April 17, 1953, Secret, GPT MIN-2, in *FRUS*, 1952-4, 443-7, 446.

might be unfavourable to the extent that it would further complicate French ratification of the EDC."[194]

Into 1953, the issue of war crimes and crimes against humanity become hindrances and obstacles to be removed and confined to memory. As the diplomatic traffic from the State Department correspondence shows, the Germany of 1953 was desperate to demarcate boundaries, and erase those 500 or so reminders of atrocity still in U.S. prisons. "Is it not time at last to draw a line under the whole account [on war criminals]?" urged Erich Dombrowski in the *Frankfurter Allgemeine Zeitung*. "Five hundred. Just a figure? Or human beings, most of whom are aware only of the fact that they did their duty?"[195] The perpetrators of atrocity were humanised, agents abiding by the call of duty, an inexorable process that the Eisenhower administration found hard to stop.

That same month, Reber informed his superiors that, "Rank and file German opinion appears almost unanimous that trial and continued imprisonment of war criminals by occupying powers somehow improper. Parallels to American actions in Korea, British in Malaya, French in Indo China regularly cited against unique German guilt."[196]

On August 31, 1953, six days before the Adenauer government went to the polls, the Interim Mixed Parole and Clemency Board (IMPAC) was established, dealing with war criminals within the American zone.[197] One of the embassy officials was keen to point out the successes of the previous board. It "had a splendid record of achievement and that due to its efforts the agitation here in Germany about war criminals has quietened down." The priorities were now in publicising the formation of a new board to take the process even further. "Germans very anxious to be able to announce further progress Parole and Clemency Board for War Criminals before election ... Is there any chance that we can announce names U.S. members selected for

---

[194] Counselor of Department of State (MacArthur), Memo of conversation at White House, Washington, June 4, 1953, in *FRUS*, 1952-4, 469.

[195] Erich Dombrowski, "The Five Hundred," *Frankfurter Allgemeine Zeitung*, January 17, 1953, attached in Edward T. Lampson, Office of Political Affairs, HICOG, Bonn, to Department of State, Dispatch No. 2050, January 19, 1953, in Folder 321.6, Box #164, War Criminals General 1953-55, HICOG, RG 466, NARA, CP, MD.

[196] Reber, Bonn, to Secretary of State, Classified Telegram, January 27, 1953, Control No. 5697, in Folder 321.6, Box #164, War Criminals, General 1953-55, HICOG, RG 466, NARA, CP, MD.

[197] Buscher, *U.S. War Crimes Trial Program in Germany*, 83. Those mainly responsible were General Charles L. Bolte, Commander in Chief of the United States occupation forces in Europe; and James B. Conant, who became the new U.S. High Commissioner replacing McCloy.

"a service to world freedom and peace."[206] Having been targets of annihilation under the Third Reich, Jews became political options in the very nation that initiated the policy in the name of the broader "democratic" aims of the United States.

Persecuted Jews had become salvaging Jews, the Holocaust legacy reversed in the name of forward-looking objectives.

A year after the report's publication, the intensity on the part of the Germans effort to influence American perceptions on how they viewed war criminals was still unabated. One official who was responsible for negotiating further on the issue of war criminals argued that "the war criminal problem should be disposed of in an orderly but expeditious manner," namely through following "board recommendations."

The successor board to IMPAC would have to be respected, its decisions followed, even if they were not unanimous. Rejection of a majority recommendation from the board "would undoubtedly have an adverse affect on our relationship with the Germans." To expect the German soldier to serve in a new army would be "inconsistent with the honor to volunteer for service while former brother officers and soldiers are still in jail," and more to the point, would "prevent many of the best men among the former officers from enlisting in the German forces and thus lower the average quality of the professional soldier group."[207]

In 1955, there was a stark impression that the Landsberg prisoners had shed, or at the very least lightened the historical weight of their crimes, a feature that characterised the discussions between the American authorities and the citizens of the new Germany. The Archbishop of Cologne, Cardinal Joseph Frings, explained to President Eisenhower how the effluxion of time had somehow enhanced the standing of the convicts. They had "atoned for their crimes by their long imprisonment and that the crimes were committed in the confusion created by war conditions and under the pressure exerted by superior agencies."[208]

Later that year, the American embassy in Moscow was reporting confidently that the Soviets would be amenable to a release of the Spandau prisoners, though Dulles cautioned that, "Any such efforts in [modifying

[206] Alson, et al, *Germany Nine Years Later*, 9.

[207] Knox Lamb, "War Criminals," to Department of State, Foreign Service Despatch, No. 249, August 3, 1955, in Folder 321.6, War Criminals-General, 1953-1955, Box #164, HICOG, RG 466, NARA, CP, MD.

[208] Joseph Frings to Dwight D. Einsenhower, Trans., June 28, 1955, in Folder 321.6, War Criminals-General 1953-1955, Box #164, HICOG, Bonn, Security-Segregated General Records, 1953-1955, RG 466, NARA, CP, MD.

prison sentences] further would have to be fully coordinated with the British and French before approaching the Soviets."[209]

Not even the sentences in the Malmédy case were immune to modification, demonstrating how far law had been politicised for strategic gain. American officials chose not to see it as such, regarding the juridical realm as distinct from the political. The welfare of the war criminal was accepted as the welfare of a general convict in a U.S. prison cell. One of the benefits of this uniform categorisation was the grant of parole. As a copy of a press release by Dulles sought to show, "Parole is a normal and widely recognized practice in the prison administration in the United States." The release went on to stress that parole was not a modification of guilt. "It is not a form of pardon or clemency, and it does not change the sentence." Crimes of war, crimes against humanity, become analogised as domestic offences against the state. Those punished could be resocialised and take their place alongside the very citizens whom they might have been responsible for persecuting. The entire parole system was designed to enable the prisoner "to adjust to a normal life in the community while completing the service of his sentence."[210]

As far as such a notorious figure of the SS (albeit in a military role) as Sepp Dietrich was concerned, his release, Ambassador James Conant stubbornly insisted, was totally logical with standard principles of penology and sovereignty. If called before the Senate Committee for Foreign Relations, as he explained to the Assistant Secretary of State for European Affairs, he would have opined that "any war criminal who was serving a thirty-year sentence and whose record in person and plans for parole were satisfactory should be released on parole after ten years and in view of the sovereign nature of the Federal Republic of Germany."

Conant argued that a figure such as Dietrich was not "hard core," though his definition of what this meant proved vague. Only war criminals with unsatisfactory parole applications, bad prison records or crimes "such as to warrant a punishment over and above that of ten years in jail and release on parole" could be detained. Optimistically, the Ambassador was confident that the committee would be "sympathetic to the general idea of supporting the

[209] See Walmsley [Moscow] to State Department, 30 September 1955, in File 321.6, War-Criminals General, 1953-1955, Box #164, HICOG, Bonn, Security-Segregated General Records, RG 466, NARA, CP, MD; Dulles, State Department to Moscow [US Embassy], Classified Telegram, 7 October 1955, Folder 321.6, War Criminals General, 1953-1955, Box #164, HICOG, Bonn, Security-Segregated General Records, RG 466, NARA, CP, MD.

[210] Press Release in Dulles, Dept of State instruction, "War criminals," to Amembassy, Bonn, No: A-553, December 10, 1955, in Folder 321.6, War Criminals General, 1953-1955, Box #164, HICOG, Bonn, Security-Segregated General Records, RG 466, NARA, CP, MD.

Chancellor's request to have as many of the war criminals released as possible at the time when Germany is sovereign and the process of building up a new army."[211]

We can gather how significant the politicisation of the war criminal issue was by its geopolitical gravity. The release of German war criminals was given greater precedence in some circles than the equivalent granting of clemency to Japanese war criminals.

In 1955, moves to grant Japanese war criminals a blanket parole were regarded as dangerous: such a measure, warned Conant, "would have most unfortunate and drastic effect here [in Germany]." The action in occupied Japan "would mean inter alia the destruction of the parole and clemency system which has been set up in Germany and which is working quite satisfactorily."[212]

Conant continued his justifications for the revitalised Germany, purified by rites of contrition, before Harvard audiences in the Godkin lectures held later that decade.

Published in a slender collection in 1958, Conant found in Germany "the spirit of a people who have turned their back on the Nazi past."[213] He found good Germans everywhere, in the Christian Democratic Union and the SPD, parties that had restored the "moral worth" of the Republic.

In what seemed to foreshadow the German historical debate in the 1980s, triggered by the salvos of historians Ernst Nolte and Andreas Hillgruber, Conant found heroic Germans in the life of the Third Reich, "active resistance groups, and those who were silent in opposition".[214]

The lectures played a brand of victim politics to the hilt: the lack of uprisings against Hitler was not justified on the basis of complicity with the executioner's creed, but bound up in fear and oppression. In the Third Reich of Conant's description, finding execrated executioners became problematic; the victims were less exclusive, since they were everywhere.

They were most certainly not just Jews. The parables of German victim of totalitarianism were recorded, as Conant noted in the lectures, in the works of

---

211 James B. Conant [Bonn] to Livingstone T. Merchant, Assistant Secretary of State for European Affairs, State Department [Washington], December 20, 1955, in Folder 321.6, War Criminals General, 1953-1955, Box #164, HICOG, Bonn, Security-Segregated General Records, RG 466, NARA, CP, MD.

212 Conant to State Department, Classified Telegram, No. 4348, 22 Jan 1955, in Folder 321. War Criminals – General, 1953-1955, RG 466, NARA, CP, MD.

213 James B. Conant, *Germany and Freedom: The Godkin Lectures at Harvard University* (Cambridge, MA: Harvard University Press, 1958), 10.

214 Conant, *Germany and Freedom*, 16.

such authors as the Eton College Master Robert Birley.[215] The base of victim politics had been broadened.

A Snapshot: The 1960s and 1970s

By the 1960s, it was evident that the Final Solution in American political responses to Germany failed to figure with any force. The framing of its legacy was not something of value in the relationship building of Bonn and Washington. The atrocities against Jews and the images of the concentration camp were transferred to the more pressing threats posed by communism and a belligerent Soviet Union. This set the scene for the irritation caused by one of America's foremost war journalists William Shirer. By the 1960s, when the controversial book *The Third Reich* reached American audiences, the historical responses to Nazi atrocities had been tranquilised by Cold war motifs and rhetoric. Felix Morley, who had preferred political executions to legalised ones in 1945, argued in 1961 that Shirer's thesis elected one form of dictatorship over the other through ascribing a "near monopoly on original sin" to the Germans.[216] The conservative American journal *Modern Age* promoted the West German and American alliance through diminishing the specter of the savage German with that of the threatening Soviet. "[O]ne would not believe it after reading Shirer ... we are living in 1962, not in 1942, and the threat to our national security does not come from Germany".[217] Brown University Professor Klaus Epstein criticised Shirer's work for applying broad criminal assumptions to the German populace. "[Edmund] Burke did not know how to draw an indictment against an entire people; Shirer does."[218]

Shirer's discussion on the Third Reich, while receiving damaging reviews in the German press, revealed how powerful the influence of Cold War reorientations had been. A sizeable body of intellectual work availed itself for Shirer's cause, revitalising the discourse on atrocities dealing with the subject of World War II. According to an academic from University of Toronto, "The

[215] Conant, *Germany and Freedom*, 18.

[216] Felix Morley, "Those Incorrigible Germans," *Modern Age* (Spring, 1961): 193, quoted in Gavriel D. Rosenfield, "The Reception of William L. Shirer's *The Rise and Fall of the Third Reich* in the United States and West Germany, 1960-2," *Journal of Contemporary History* 29 (1994): 95-128, 108.

[217] William Henry Chamberlain, "The Rise and Fall of the Third Reich," *Modern Age* (Summer, 1962), 83, quoted in Rosenfeld, "Shirer's *Rise and Fall of the Third Reich*," 109.

[218] Klaus Epstein, "Shirer's History of Nazi Germany," *Review of Politics* 23, 2 (April, 1961): 230-45, 242.

Nuremberg Trials (amid growing doubts about their legal foundation) faded into the category of ancient history, the disagreeable, the irrelevant past."[219] Shirer's work served to rescue the "twelve-year nightmare" that had disappeared "in the wake of cold war" through recording "the horrors of this mindless regime, recorded as only modern barbarism can be" thereby recapitulating evident truths about totalitarianism for a Western audience numbed by political amnesia.[220]

English professor Geoffrey Barraclough's review in *The Nation* argued that the memories of the Third Reich had somehow lost their "reality" to the public. "Other events have dulled the shock that stirred our consciousness when the Nuremberg trials brought the foulness of the Nazis in to full light."[221] Within the milieu of cultural amnesia, Shirer and Barraclough were "the club bores of the sixties" having witnessed the consequences of the Great War: "no one wants to listen to us, and people whisper that we are obsessed, hysterical and anti-German."[222] Criticisms by such scholars as Epstein on the continuity of German militarism were not accurate: Hitler was not "an unhappy accident", an abnormal condition of German history.

Most depressing for Barraclough were attempts to peck away at Nuremberg's legacy, the failure to accurately carry out the realisation in Germany of the historical threat posed by the Hitler phenomenon. Those responsible for atrocities still lay waiting, concealed by the political climate of the day. On the next visit to Germany, the tourist might be sitting "next to a gas-chamber thug on the bus; and that fat woman guzzling cakes in the *Konditorei* may be an erstwhile murderess from Ravensbruck."[223] A letter to the *Nation* editors from a Chicago reader concurred, not feeling inhibited by the Burkeian puzzle of indictable nations. Barraclough and Shirer's indictment of the German people was "historically accurate." It was "tragic" that America's "policy makers, in the interests of expediency, turn their backs on the obvious fact."[224]

One would have thought that Shirer's work would not have resonated at the international level, a tome that could hardly damage a nation's credibility.

---

[219] John C. Cairns, "The Rise and Fall of the Third Reich," *International Journal* 16, 2 (Spring, 1961): 188-9, 188.

[220] Cairns, "Rise and Fall," 188-9.

[221] Geoffrey Barraclough, "Hitler in Cinerama," *The Nation* 191, 14 (October 29, 1960): 330-1, 330.

[222] Barraclough, "Hitler," 330. A similar view was expressed by A. J. P. Taylor, who swore never to set foot on German soil for fear of shaking the hand of one accused of atrocities: see discussion in *A Personal History* (London: Hamish Hamilton, 1983).

[223] Barraclough, "Hitler," 330.

[224] Meyer Goldman, "Irrefutable Truth," *The Nation* 191, 16 (November 12, 1960): 356.

But sensitive German readers disagreed. Such matters as the Holocaust were unnecessary intrusions in the U.S.-German relationship. Adenauer, seeing another election on the horizon in the early 1960s, tried to scotch the supposed influence the book was having on American perceptions of Germany. He also had, as a State Department assessment observes, other worries on his mind before his visit to the United States: the growing influence of perceived anti-German sentiment in light of the Republic's resurgent foreign policy and increasing brazenness, and the Eichmann Trial.[225]

At the receipt of his Aspen award in 1978, McCloy was no wiser on the Holocaust's role in U.S.-German relations, where the politics of the executioner had overwhelmed the moral legacy of the victims. The politics of the Holocaust victim was regarded as the politics of negativity and pessimism. Ironically, if Heinrich Himmler saw the mass murdering of Jews as "an unwritten and never to be written page of glory in our history," the problem of situating the memory of Jewish suffering in US-German relations during the early part of the Cold War lay in precisely these same unutterable dimensions.[226] As the "accidental remnant," to use Emile Fackenheim's words, Jewish survivors, and those who did not survive, failed to register as forceful measures in the battle for memories.

The crimes of the Holocaust were in effect de-radicalized by conventional laws and conventional punishments. The entire abnormality of crimes against humanity became normalised through conventional penological principles: parole and prisoner welfare, administered through sympathetic boards of review. This result had much to do with the way the offences were tried; genocide had not materialised as a specific crime – the UN Genocide Convention would only criminalize it in 1948. Crimes against humanity were still seen as unorthodox, but they only served to punish with the broad rhetoric of civilization, thereby attempting to remain conventional. The crimes of the Holocaust (at least in the political discourse of the early Cold War) were thus not seen as exceptional. This was exemplified perhaps by Bonn's classification of released war criminals as conventional prisoners of war. American responses to the Holocaust in the occupied territories of Germany were not a matter of mastering the past but conquering the precarious future.

---

225 "Scope Paper." [1961] 9 pgs. Secret. Declassified. Issued: April 12, 1961, Presidential Security File, Government Agencies, State Department, 1962-63, Lyndon Baines Johnson Library, Austin, Texas.

226 Quoted in Richard Breitman, *The Architect of Genocide: Himmler and the Final Solution* (London: Bodley Head, 1991), 243.

Chapter 3

THE EICHMANN TRIAL

A "LAWLESS" ACT OR THE "QUIET VOICE OF WESTERN JUSTICE"?

The Eichmann Trial began with a lawless act.
Yosal Rogat,
The Eichmann Trial, 24.

The three judges are still the quiet voices of Western justice.
P. O'Donovan,
New Republic, May 15, 1961, 8.

On Garibaldi Street in the San Fernando section of Buenos Aires, a man by the name of Ricardo Klement was walking home unusually late one evening in March 1960, holding a bouquet of flowers. The bus he normally took had been delayed. Burly men were patiently observing Klement's movements to the claps of thunder. Their quarry was also unusual. It was Adolf Eichmann.[227]

In April 1961, Michael Gordon arrived at his work at Jerry's Liquor on East Charleston Boulevard in Las Vegas and noticed "on his plywood ... container alongside his liquor store the words 'free Eichmann'."

---

[227] Accounts of his capture can be found in Moshe Pearlman, *The Capture of Adolf Eichmann* (London: Weidenfeld and Nicolson, 1961); Ian Black and Benny Morris, *Israel's Secret Wars: A History of Israel's Intelligence Services* (New York: Grove Weidenfeld, 1991); and Isser Harel, *The House on Garibaldi Street* (London: Frank Cass, 1997).

He promptly reported this to the Federal Bureau of Investigation.[228]

The capture of Eichmann by Israel's daring Mossad agents and his subsequent trial in Jerusalem in 1961 advertised the Holocaust in an unprecedented manner to global audiences. It enabled the State of Israel to make an argument for the existence of world complicity in the destruction of Jews.[229] In the words of the party organ of David Ben-Gurion's Mapai party *Davar*, "not only Nazi Germany was responsible for the destruction of six million Jews."[230] But what did it do to American opinions of the fledgling state and perceptions of the Holocaust in a foreign theatre?

Historiography on the subject suggests that the Eichmann episode engendered sympathy and admiration, placing Israel on the road towards what would become a 'special relationship' with Washington. Such a contention is, however, a difficult one to make, given the controversy the capture, trial, and ultimate execution caused in the United States. The Israeli state was, in one sense, respected as a brave international citizen keen on avenging the death of millions, mindful of international law yet unconstrained by its more rigid requirements (the law against kidnapping for instance). In another, it was a law breaker, indifferent to established rules of international order. Various public commentators saw the criticism levelled at the legality of the trial as unduly positivist.[231] International laws that proved rigid, unduly restraining in their moral vacuity, would have allowed an individual of Eichmann's stature to go unpunished, finding fault in the form of his capture, rather than the substance of his crimes. Out of the controversial flotsam of American debate on the subject of Eichmann's capture came contrasting views on the politics of punishing the perpetrator of mass crimes against humanity. American reaction was deeply divided on the subject. Israel featured at stages as the careful law-abiding citizen, enforcing justice through trial and punishment, even towards such a singular criminal as Eichmann. But Israel also came across as careless, vindictive and disrespectful of international law. Periodicals, depending on

---

228 SAC, Las Vegas, to Director, FBI, Memorandum, 25 April 1961. Subject "Adolf Eichmann, Information Concerning." Folder 65-65842, Sec. 1, 1 of 3, Box #25, Class 65, RG 65, Records Relating to Espionage [Records of the Federal Bureau of Investigation, Class Files, 1929-1969], National Archives and Records Administration (NARA), College Park (CP), MD.

229 See Hannah Arendt, *Eichmann in Jerusalem: A Report on the Banality of Evil*, Rev. Version (New York: Penguin Books, 1994; orig. 1963), 9; David S. Wyman, "The United States," in D. Wyman, ed., *The World Reacts to the Holocaust* (Baltimore, MD: Johns Hopkins University Press, 1996), 726; and see David Cesarini, *Eichmann: His Life and Crimes* (London: William Heinemann, 2004).

230 Quoted in Arendt, *Eichmann in Jerusalem*, 9.

231 Gary Dunford, "The Eichmann Trial," Letters, *Saturday Review*, 44 (April 29, 1961): 21.

their political, even religious orientation, varied in temper and approach. American Christian publications and various public figures urged mercy; progressive journals argued for legal propriety. Conservative periodicals like the *National Review*, today as pro-Israeli as any publication in the U.S., argued that Israel could do well without this trial, calling it a nationalist, even dangerous indulgence. Nor was such a legal procedure free, as the Israeli authorities claimed, of political machinations and strategic interests. Those very same interests had governed U.S. policies on war crimes in Germany and Japan.[232]

The trial's legal critics took issue with the parochial aspect of the trial. Former U.S. Counsel at Nuremberg, Telford Taylor, sagaciously wondered whether Israel was the appropriate forum for trial and punishment. Would it not have been more prescient to stage the trial in Germany, where it might have a greater effect, rather than a state which did not exist when Eichmann's crimes were committed? In effect, this is exactly what happened when the Auschwitz-Frankfurt trials were conducted, with extensive publicity in Germany.[233] His criticism suggested a different interpretation of the Holocaust, one fostered by Nuremberg's universalizing rhetoric of guarding all humanity against state terror.[234] Trials, Taylor implied, should not be parochial expressions of racial identity or national image; they should instead find form in a scrupulous balancing of the interests of the accused and those of the victim. One reader of the *Saturday Review* insisted that what was perpetrated against the Jews was not unique, being part of a more collective evil, a general, rather than singular lesson of history. "It is more significant that Eichmann's crimes were perpetrated against humanity than that they were perpetrated against one particular group."[235]

ISRAEL AND THE HIGHER LAW

The treatment of Eichmann by the Israeli authorities suggests the elevation of the Holocaust into the realm of exceptionality. Eichmann's legal team had

---

232 See debates between Nathan Davidson and F. Lohenbill, "The Disgrace of the Eichmann Trial," *Contemporary Issues* 48 (Spring, 1964): 8-9.

233 This was notably dramatized in Peter Weiss, *Ermittlung* or *The Investigation: A Play* (New York: Atheneum, 1966); Emmi Bonhoeffer, *Auschwitz Trials: Letters from an Eye Witness*, trans. Ursula Stechow (Richmond: John Knox Press, 1967).

234 On this distinction see Lawrence Douglas, *The Memory of Judgment: Making Law and History in the Trials of the Holocaust* (New Haven: Yale University Press, 2001), 178.

235 John Pizer, "The Eichmann Trial," Letters, *Saturday Review* 44 (April 29, 1961): 21.

argued that international law knew of no such category, and that the powers of the Israeli legislature had been exceeded.[236] The victims, countered the prosecution, required avenging; and the laws had to bend to reflect that purpose. Israel, according to its mercurial leader Ben-Gurion, was a state higher than law itself. Its interests were sovereign over conventional norms of international agreement: there was no law higher than the moral state of Israel in the pursuit of the enemy of the Jewish people. The very act of wronging the Jews entitled the State of Israel, embodied with the spirit of the dead, to try its enemies within this state of exceptional jurisprudence.

American audiences were barraged with frequent pleas and commentaries by Israeli commentators about this exceptional case. As Ben-Gurion's piece in the *New York Times Magazine* proclaimed, "it is historic justice that [Eichmann] be tried by a Jewish state. Only a Jewish state can try him, from a moral point of view." The Final Solution was the incomparable atrocity that transcended the obstructing barriers of sovereignty and statehood. "Those brothers and sisters were murdered by Eichmann and who undertook to search him out were right morally although perhaps not formally. I know they committed a breach of the law, but sometimes there are moral obligations higher than formal law."[237] The legal proceedings were undertaken in their name, not that of Eichmann. "The trial is not necessary for the defendant," explained one member of the Knesset in August 1960. "It is necessary because we need to remind the world of what happened during World War II, something they would like to consign to an oblivion."[238]

Eichmann's Israeli prosecutor Gideon Hausner wrote a three-part account of his views of the trial in the *Saturday Evening Post* in November 1962. American readers were exposed to the significance of the event. For the first time, "Jews had a chance to bring an oppressor to justice".[239] There were crucial observations to the evolution of a Holocaust consciousness: in distinction to Nuremberg, for instance, the trial was specifically undertaken in the name of Jews. Hausner even rebuked Nuremberg for its universal legal ideal, an ideal that was made to forgo the particularism of Jewish suffering in favour of broader humanitarian ideals. "In none of these [Nuremberg] trials

---

[236] Discussion in *The Attorney-General of the Government of Israel v Eichmann*, Criminal Case No 40/61, Dec 11, 1961, discussed in Covey Oliver, " Judicial Decisions," The American Journal of International Law 56, 3 (Jul,. 1962): 802-845, 802.

[237] *New York Times Magazine*, December 18, 1960.

[238] August 8, 1960, *Knesset Proceedings* 29, 2106. See also Elie Wiesel, "Eichmann's Victims and the Unheard Testimony," *Commentary* 32 (December, 1961): 510-6

[239] Gideon Hausner, "Eichmann and his Trial," *Saturday Evening Post* 235, 41 (November 17, 1962): 85-90, 85 (herein part III).

[...] was the Jewish tragedy – the systematic killing of at least 6,000,000 human beings, one third of the Jewish people – the core of the indictment."[240]

This reaction was mimicked in some American periodicals, including religious journals troubled by how a trial of Eichmann might be justified. His legal status, went one contribution in the Christian publication *Commonweal*, was of less consequence, despite the writer's concession that "the manner of Eichmann's capture and the trial itself raises many troubling questions of international law." None of these factors could obfuscate the "central fact behind the trial," namely, that "nineteen hundred years after the birth of Christ, a monstrous form of barbarity arose in the heart of Christian Europe." The exceptional station of the victims, not the legal status of the perpetrator, had to be remembered: "Whatever else is said about the Eichmann trial, it is surely right that we who are Christian remember the six million men, women and children who were coldly and systematically put to death because they were Jews."[241]

Significantly, Eichmann's punishment came to be seen as a necessary legal exorcism, an act of normative jurisprudence. Far from being a rights holder, the German suspect had thrown away the shield protecting his innocence till trial. Criticisms of Ben-Gurion's Israel emanated from, in the words of one letter writer from Brooklyn, "super-legalistic and morally offended technicalists".[242] No one, whether a "legally constituted body", nation or "duly established authority" had sought Eichmann, who was as good as condemned, a "defiler of God and murderer of millions."[243] A reader of the *Saturday Review* from Washington D.C. similarly found Israel as the most suitable venue to try Eichmann, given the presence of "300,000 survivors of his 'final solution' who are potential witnesses, and of the most extensive documentation in existence".[244]

A former advisor to Israel's UN delegation Jacob Robinson expressed the same view in the American Jewish Association's flagship journal *Commentary*. Practical considerations and expertise were obviously in Israel's favour. "Israel is surely the best place for trying Eichmann. There are ... 300,000 ... survivors, the greatest concentration of potential witnesses anywhere, the most exclusive documentation".[245]

---

[240] Hausner, "Eichmann," Part III, 85.
[241] James O'Gara, "The Eichmann Case," *Commonweal* 174 (May 12, 1961): 166.
[242] William Sunners, "No Other Cared," *New York Times Magazine*, January 22, 1961, 30.
[243] Sunners, "No Other Cared," 30.
[244] Charles Kanner, "The Eichmann Trial," Letters, *Saturday Review* 44 (April 29, 1961): 21.
[245] "Eichmann and the Problem of Jurisdiction," *Commentary* 30 (1960): 1.

What we find in such reactions is a redrawing, one might even say withdrawal of the executioner's rights in the Holocaust. The comments of one of the trial's most vocal supporters, Pennsylvania Supreme Court justice Michael A. Musmano prove illustrative. For Musmano, the balancing of rights had to be skewed away from the executioner. "In urging the rights of Adolf Eichmann, many commentators, essayists and speakers completely ignored the rights of the slain."[246] For Musmano, as indeed for fellow believers in the politics of the Holocaust victim, only Israel had the power to "speak for the six million murdered Jews", notwithstanding its non-existence at the time of the atrocities.[247]

An extension of highlighting the victim in the political discourse on Eichmann was the favourable response to Israel, whose muscular assertiveness in abducting Eichmann was seen in some quarters as the triumphant culmination of a wounded people. In much commentary on the trial Jewish culture is flattered, the state of Israel respected. Some research into public reactions to the trial at the time shows a more sympathetic disposition towards the fate of the Jewish people, who are both modern victims yet heroic victors who triumphed with the establishment of the State of Israel. According to one study done a few years after the trial, "The reaction of Americans to the Eichmann trial can be summarized as one of interest and of a trend toward increased sympathy for Israel and Jews."[248]

Significantly, through dramatizing and politicizing the Holocaust at the Eichmann trial, Israel became, in American political discourses, a protector of the 'free world.' The Holocaust was seen as the outcome of a totalitarian system, a result that was not necessarily consistent with Hausner's attempt to singularise the atrocities committed against Jews (he was hardly referring to all forms of totalitarianism in his presentation). For the jurist Musmano, the trial was specific in "serving notice on all world Jewbaiters and haters as to what will await them if they ever attempt to put into execution their latent and patent malignancies."[249]

But it was far more than that. The punishment of Eichmann was a godsend for the American way of life. One commentator in a Washington-based paper

---

[246] Michael A. Musmano, "The Objections Intimine to the Eichmann Trial," *Temple Law Quarterly* 35, 1 (Fall 1961): 1-22, 17.

[247] Musmano, "Objections," 14.

[248] Irving Crespi, "Public Reaction to the Eichmann Trial," *Public Opinion Quarterly* 28 (Spring, 1964): 91-103, 101.

[249] Michael A. Musmano, "At the Eichmann Trial," Address at Luncheon of Federation of Jewish Agencies of Greater Philadelphia, Warwick Hotel, June 13, 1961, printed in *Congressional Record*, Appendix, 87 Congress, 1st Sess. (1961): A4986-4988, 4986.

argued that, "Anyone who had seen all of that [described in the Trial] will oppose all the rest of his life any Fascist or Communist groups which seek to dilute American freedom by fanatic attacks on our courts, our constitution, and our individual liberty."[250] The Anti-Defamation League argued that Israel, in trying Eichmann, was undertaking a moral mission "to alert the conscience of the world to the fearful consequences of totalitarianism."[251] Senator Hubert Humphrey of Minnesota regarded the trial as "a potent reminder of the end results of a totalitarian system whether it be fascist or communist." Israel was in a sense the guardian of the free world through punishing the Holocaust perpetrator, giving resolve "to strengthen us in our determination to preserve our free and democratic society."[252]

THE VOICE OF JUSTICE

Some political notables praised Israel, giving short shrift to any suggestion that Eichmann could not be tried fairly. Governor David L. Lawrence of Pennsylvania was a true admirer, describing Israel in a speech to the Statewide Israel Histadrut Campaign Dinner in May 1961 as a land without flaws, pristine in its moral aims, filled with "the glorious, sunlit promise of the future" and a society with "love and respect for law." For Lawrence, it was essential for Israel to bring to the fore the memory of the victims, essential since the "memory of man" was "brief," and busily closing "a final door on the atrocities men commit against themselves." In time, he feared the possibility that "our grandchildren would see the Nazis as a heroic breed of fighter." In the trial, the true relevance of Israel was revealed, as a nation that had redeemed the memory of the victims - those six million "witnesses" who could not testify in the courtroom - through punishment. "For today ... we begin to see the true greatness of a people whose love of justice surpasses all personal thirst for vengeance."[253]

Senator Jacob Javits, at the conclusion of the trial, was satisfied that the proceeding "was conducted with impeccable justice, as the world had a right

[250] Ralph McGill, "The Passing Scene – The Eichmann Trial's Bizarre Tone," *Evening Star*, April 17, 1961.

[251] Quoted in Novick, *Holocaust and Collective Memory*, 132.

[252] Hubert H. Humphrey, *Congressional Record*, Appendix, 87 Congress, 1st Sess., 107 (April 1961): A2577.

[253] David L. Lawrence, Remarks at Statewide Israel Histradrut Campaign Dinner, Sheraton Hotel, Philadelphia, Pa., May 28, 1961, in *Congressional Record*, Appendix, 87 Congress, 1st Sess., 107 (June 1960): A4091.

to expect from Israel." But Israel had done more than issue a verdict of justice: it had given humanity a precedent against the bureaucratic perpetrator of atrocities: "that he [humanity] cannot escape his [its] personal responsibility for violation of the laws of humanity by incriminating others by claiming superior orders or by pleading fear."[254]

Others felt that Israel could not err in its actions on this issue. In a speech by Congressman Victor L. Anfuso, delivered at the Concorde Hotel in New York some months after the abduction, Israel was seen as above error –"the people of Israel are not capable of an injustice and I am sure they will give Eichmann a fair trial." Even before the proceedings, Anfuso, having ignored the irritating "legalisms" of the case, predicted a trial "guided by the supreme Judaic concept of justice." This concept of justice was steeped in the legacy of "the prophets," guided by the "wisdom of a Solomon". For Anfuso, the Jews as victims would disseminate the justice of the victim, though he concluded by wishing that the Israeli government allow "an international genocide committee" to try him.[255]

Such views were echoed by a member of the Californian Bar, Zad Leavy. The judges who condemned Eichmann had positioned themselves not far from the ancient Supreme Court of the Jews, whose usages had somehow "found its way through universal acceptance into modern jurisprudence to guide orderly conduct amongst men."[256]

Some journalists and essayists were sympathetic and impressed with Israel as the scrupulous punisher. In the words of a *New York Post* editorial, "The highest judge and the lowliest magistrate will be reminded that in this Israeli courtroom a new nation affirmed the right of the lowliest of the species to full judicial process."[257] Even if the abduction had somehow left a "bad taste" for those keen positivists guided by "rules for peaceful conduct among themselves [men and nations]," the trial itself was a "noteworthy step towards acceptance of principles which someday may be the basis of peace and good order among nations."[258] Israel, the law-driven society, had been instrumental in allowing law to assume a "leadership" role in an age where genocide could occur in a

[254] Jacob Javits, "The Eichmann Verdict," *Congressional Record*, 87th Congress, 2d Sess., 108, pt. 1, January 17, 1962, 361-2, 361.

[255] Address by Victor L. Anfuso, Grand Master's Dinner, Order Brith Abraham, Concord Hotel, Kiamesha Lake, N.Y., June 28, 1960, *Congressional Record*, 86 Cong, 2d Sess., 106, pt. 12, July 2, 1960, 15865-6, 15866.

[256] Zad Leavy, " The Eichmann Trial and the Role of Law," *American Bar Association Journal* 48, 9 (September 1962): 820-5, 820.

[257] *New York Post*, "The Lesson of Eichmann," August 7, 1961.

[258] Leavy, "The Eichmann Trial," 822, 824.

matter of "minutes".[259] Martha Gellhorn, who had vividly described the "skeletons" of Dachau for her readership, was "shocked" at suggestions that "the whole [trial] was useless," leaving only malignant anti-Semitism in its wake. "The trial was essential, to every human being now alive, and to all who follow us ... This is the best record we and our descendants will ever have; and we owe the state of Israel an immeasurable debt for providing it." In short, Israel was instructing humanity in the classroom of history, for "we are obliged to learn from [the trial], for the safety and honor of the species."[260] It was impossible, reasoned Gellhorn, to comprehend "the complete dimensions of twentieth-century man – and that includes all of us, I insist – without studying the Eichmann Trial."

Israel as a Monopolizing Voice

Many commentators disagreed with Ben-Gurion's assessment of Israeli exceptionalism, their opinions formed along various views of the political divide. The assumption of speaking for the victims through the medium of Israeli justice riled American Jews who felt threatened by the Premier's assumption of moral authority on their behalf. That any Jews in the United States would dissent from the trial was interesting, for a battle was being waged not merely over the politics of victims and perpetrators in Holocaust discourse, but a battle over how those victims were to be avenged. Clarence L. Coleman, Jr., President of the American Council for Judaism, wrote to U.S. Secretary of State Christopher A. Herter arguing that Ben-Gurion had been unreasonable in assuming that Israel was "the only sovereign authority in Jewry" with the power "to see that the whole of this story, in all its horror, is fully explained."[261]

The implications of Israel's actions, warned Coleman, were rooted in a fundamentally Zionist conception of Israel's global role, based on "dangerous motivations" in representing "the citizens of other countries on the sole ground of their identification with Jews."[262] This case was also argued by Alfred Kazin in the *Reporter*, who found the fusion of victim politics with the credo

[259] Leavy, "The Eichmann Trial," 825.

[260] Gellhorn, "Eichmann and the Private Conscience," 53-4.

[261] Quoting Ben-Gurion in Clarence L. Coleman to Christopher A. Herter, "Eichmann Case Raises Old Question: Can Israel Speak for All Jews?" *Issues* 14, 6 (Summer, 1960): 65-9, 66.

[262] Coleman, "Old Question," 67.

of Zionism dangerously close to the very the totalitarian ideologies Jews had perished to. Ben-Gurion, Kazin argued, spoke of "Jews [who] have no future except in Israel – catastrophically similar to totalitarian arguments about the 'Decline of the West' and dangerously shortsighted, since Israel is not likely to survive if the Jews do not survive elsewhere."[263]

Various papers cited by Coleman saw the identity politics of Israel's assertions disturbing, even to American concepts of sovereignty. All anti-Semitic crimes, warned the *Chicago Daily News*, would see Israel "qualified to take criminal jurisdiction over injustices to all Jews anywhere in the world."[264] The Boston *Herald* disputed Israel's assertion as being "the only authority on Jewry." By Ben-Gurion's statements, "all anti-Semitic crimes perpetrated in the United States would cease to be the responsibility of our own law enforcement and become those of Israeli 'volunteers'."[265] The *Washington Post* argued that Israel's ethnic appropriations of world Jewry would do "a grave disservice to Jews of other nationalities."[266] Coleman rounded off his letter against Israel, and its role as the only voice of the Holocaust victims, by raising the barricades. Herter was reminded that Washington was "legally obligated to protect its U.S. citizens of Jewish faith against this clear policy of Zionism and Israel to establish claims of representation and of moral stewardship over all Jews."[267]

ISRAEL AS OUTLAW

The higher law pronounced by Ben-Gurion was a fiction for legal positivists and black-letter lawyers concerned with Eichmann's legal welfare. In the opinion of one Constitutional jurist Yosal Rogat, the law as it stood was actually retarded by the actions of Israel, in that it was mistaken to disregard the existing conventions in favour of extra-judicial actions.[268] Rogat's essay, published by the Centre for Democratic Institutions, a body with prominent members of America's intellectual elite, found Israel's anti-juridical approach deeply flawed. On the one hand, Israel "assimilated the Eichmann Trial to a compelling tradition which goes back at least to Antigone – that which holds

[263] Alfred Kazin, "Eichmann and the New Israelis," *The Reporter* 24 (April 27, 1961): 24-5.
[264] Quoted in Coleman, "Old Question," 67.
[265] Quoted in Coleman, "Old Question," 67.
[266] Quoted in Coleman, "Old Question," 67.
[267] Coleman, "Old Question," 69.
[268] Yosal Rogat, *The Eichmann Trial and the Rule of Law* (Santa Barbara, Calif.: Center for the Study of Democratic Institutions, Fund for the Republic, November 1961), 32.

that higher purposes must sometimes be paramount if they conflict with formal rules of law."[269] On the other, it was radical and destabilizing.

Rogat's reasoning approached the Final Solution in a different light: that a parochial trial conducted in its shadow would diminish the role of international law. Israel's "decision that she alone should try Eichmann for crimes against Jews rather than having an international tribunal try him for crimes against human beings ... retards efforts to apply the rule of law to the international community."[270] The difference in Rogat's language was no accident: the exceptionalism of victimhood in Israel's legal rhetoric prejudiced broader applications of international law, undermining the international polity with notions of vengeful nationalism. "It is perhaps the greatest irony of the trial that its two antagonistic forces – Israel and the Nazis – have both asserted the older view of membership and identity."[271] Other lawyers such as Robert K. Woetzel were of similar mind. Being "tried by a court of a state which did not exist at the time that the acts were committed, outside of the territory where they took place, and under a retroactive law, does not enhance the standing of law in the proceeding."[272]

Then there was Telford Taylor, the key American prosecutor of Nazi crimes at Nuremberg, who found glaring procedural defects in the trial. Israel was playing the legal game heavy-handedly, ignoring basic rights. It worried him that "no Israeli lawyer was willing to undertake the defence."[273] The trial could have been undertaken as an "inquest" rather than a "prosecution"; the Israeli Government had pre-judged Eichmann's guilt, a "premise" that "stultifie[d] the entire discussion."[274] Taylor regarded the treatment of Eichmann as a poor precedent for international law, tried "in a land to which he had been brought by clandestine force," based upon an "absolute nationalism which is irreconcilable with the very idea of international law".[275]

Hans Zeisel at the University of Chicago Law School, a regular contributor to Jewish periodicals at the time, considered the trial of limited sociological utility: "how is one to pay for Auschwitz?" His answer came in the form of an insipid Viennese joke: if ever the Führer were to face a Jew in a

---

269 Rogat, *Eichmann Trial*, 5.
270 Rogat, *Eichmann Trial*, 41.
271 Rogat, *Eichmann Trial*, 21.
272 Robert K. Woetzel, *The Nuremberg Trials in International Law with a Postlude on the Eichmann Case* (New York: Frederick A. Praeger, Inc., 1962), 258.
273 Telford Taylor, "Large Questions in the Eichmann Case," *New York Times Magazine*, January 22, 1961: 11, 22-5, 22.
274 Taylor, "Large Questions," 25, 23
275 Taylor, "Large Questions," 22.

coffee shop, the German leader, eager to read the paper in the latter's possession, would be refused: "[Hitler] will then ask me 'May I please borrow your newspapers?' And I shall look straight at him and say 'No not you Herr Hitler!'" [276] Rogat's discussion went along similar lines. "By trying Eichmann for a crime, and by simplifying the account [of his character and motives], Israel suggested an analogy to ordinary legal phenomena."[277]

Lawyers speculated that the Eichmann precedent could produce its zealous imitators, anarchic citizens charging through sovereign borders with their abducted quarry to settle scores. One commentary published in the *American Journal of International Law* just after the abduction on the issue of Croatian war criminals in the United States pondered the issue. The spectacle of "a group of Serbs, inspired by hatred, revenge, and patriotism" whisking away war crime suspects of the former Croatian government was not a fanciful one.[278] With irony, the author reflected that, as Eichmann went on trial, "we can only hope that our consciences will rest easy because we can point to [Andrija] Artukovic, in his haven in California, as a symbol of our devotion to government of law and not of men."[279]

Some members of press opinion found Israel's legal adventurousness distasteful. A notable and consistent critic of Israel's action vis-à-vis its role as a good citizen of international law was the *Jewish Newsletter*, a periodical edited by the psychoanalyst Erich Fromm, with a circulation in New York. The *Newsletter* published opinions critical of Israel's failure to conquer the moral divide that the Holocaust had seemingly opened. Fromm argued as much in an early June issue, arguing that Israel had simply copied its sworn enemy: "the kidnapping of Eichmann is an act of lawlessness of exactly the type of which the Nazis themselves (and the Stalin and Trujillo regimes) have been guilty." The spectre of immoral Nazism, far from being distanced and particularised in the proceedings, had been brought closer to home, a global disease that was simply reasserting itself in the form of a modern trauma. Eichmann's rights had been unequivocally violated, damaging the Israeli case against him. "The State of Israel has failed to conquer the Nazi spirit by not rising to a higher moral attitude than that of lawless revenge."[280]

[276] Zeisel, "Who Are the Guilty?" 50.

[277] Rogat, *Eichmann Trial*, 13.

[278] Michael H. Cordozo, *AJIL* 55 (1961): 127-135, 127.

[279] Cardozo note, 135. Artukovic, a notorious member of the Pavlevic regime in Croatia, was accused for crimes against humanity.

[280] Erich Fromm, "Israel and World Jews," *Jewish Newsletter*, 16, 13 (June 2, 1960), unpaginated.

In late June, the *Newsletter* published the warnings of Congressional House representative Stuyvesant Wainwright. Whilst feeling no love for Eichmann, Wainwright found the process of kidnapping disruptive to the image of Israel as a law-abiding citizen. "I feel that Eichmann should perish by the sword – but by the sword of justice rather than through the kidnapping process." The act of kidnapping "will leave a black mark on the Israeli Government's respect for law and order."[281] The *Newsletter* further noted the negative reactions from some diplomatic sources in the U.S. State Department concerned with the Middle East. The kidnapping, in the words of an unnamed diplomat, had a sinister tone to it, and would convince critics of Israel in the region about Zionism's true purpose.[282]

Christian publications were also wondering if Israel had overstepped the mark in seeking, not merely to try Eichmann, but execute him. The Jesuit publication *America* was keen to exorcise the spirit of vengeance. The trial "lacked the authority, the universality, the solemnity of the great judgment passed by the Allies in 1946." Israel was modelling itself as a citizen of international law while violating it. "No amount of empathy for Jewish opinion warrants abandonment of all critical sense in weighing the significance of such unilateral actions on foreign soil." [283] "A sound and healthy world community," it noted in an editorial in July 1961, "cannot rest solidly on fear and the spirit of vengeance."[284] The following year, the journal editorialised in a manner that saw the concentration camp, its bodies, its crematoria, as hindrances to reconciliation. Talking about victims retarded hopes for the future. "Is it good psychology or good mental health to exhume, in all their sordid, criminal and tragic detail, the experiences of world Jewry at the hands of the Nazis? Can good understanding between Christian and Jew be built on such a foundation?"[285] The *Christian Century* ran pieces similarly hankering for the quality of mercy, seeing a living Eichmann as a greater service to Israeli justice than an executed one, "tempered with mercy, undeserving of it though Eichmann is."[286]

A few liberal journals were similarly reluctant to endorse Israel's hardline on Eichmann. The presumption of Eichmann's right to a fair trial struck a

[281] Stuyvesant Wainwright, "An American Congressman Speaks," *Jewish Newsletter* 16, 13 (June 27, 1960).
[282] "Israel's Motives," *Jewish Newsletter* 16, 13 (June 27, 1960), unpaginated.
[283] Editorial, "Eichmann the Christian," *America* 106 (March, 1962): 814-5, 815.
[284] "Trial of a Nazi," *America* 105 (July 29, 1961): 564, noted in Novick, *Holocaust and Collective Memory*, 313.
[285] "Eichmann the 'Christian'?" *America* 106 (March 24, 1962): 814.
[286] *Christian Century*, "Oppose the Death Penalty," 319.

chord with the *New Republic*, which claimed that Israel "would do well to confess error and hand Eichmann back to the Argentine authorities."[287] A particularly savage article by Milton Mayer, published in the *Progressive* in April 1961, satirised a conversation between Eichmann and his Israeli captor. "You mean you have 'the right' to do wrong because somebody else has done wrong to you?" The author's own version of Eichmann observed how the Israelis were, "Just like us. You know, Caesar said of his victorious troops in Gaul, 'Everyday the conquerors become more like the conquered.'" Israel could not be a judge in its own case; the victim righting its own wrong. In any case, punishing Eichmann was superfluous, a historically ineffectual gesture. Even if he was hanged "four million times," the Israeli's would have still done away with the "wrong man."[288]

Sentiment in the more mainstream publications was similarly agitated by the adduction and trial. Homer Bigart in the *New York Times* found the case for the prosecution dramatic, more theatrical than legal. "During the prosecutor's presentation, the trial appeared to be more like a folk opera than a legal case, with poets and lecturers fainting, and with much time devoted to painting the lurid background of the holocaust."[289] The *Minneapolis Star* preferred to do things by the book: return Eichmann to Argentinean authorities, seek extradition under international law, and duly inform Germany and Austria of his capture.[290] Guilty he might be argued the *Reporter*, but Israelis would have to "let others sentence him."[291] A letter writer to the *Saturday Review* from New York found the proceedings against the arraigned German as nothing more than a "Kangaroo trial" that "ought to frighten us all." The Mossad agents were "thugs" who had been "allowed to get away with kidnapping a man from one continent to stand trial on another continent for legal 'crimes' committed on a third".[292] A respondent to the *Saturday Evening Post* from North Chicago expressed puzzlement at the propriety of the entire trial. "Agreed. Eichmann was a monster. But the question is: could Israel's court legally try him? Did he have due process of law? As I see it, the trial had no semblance of reality. Even his arrest was an outright kidnapping job."[293]

[287] "Israel and the Law," *New Republic* 142 (June 20, 1961): 5.
[288] Milton Mayer, "Eichmann in Israel," *The Progressive* 25 (April, 1961): 17-20, 19-20.
[289] *New York Times*, July 3, 1961.
[290] "Israel Rejects A World Trial for Eichmann," *Daily News* (New York), June 1, 1960, 45; *Minneapolis Star*, June 8, 1960.
[291] *Reporter*, 23 (June 23, 1960): 2.
[292] Martin Henderson, "The Eichmann Trial," Letters, *Saturday Review* 44 (April 29, 1961): 21.
[293] Carl Foerster, Letter, *Saturday Evening Post* 235, 43 (December 1, 1962): 4.

Mayer's article was strident and defiant, inviting an indignant response from a former special legal consultant to the Nuremberg war crimes tribunals as "vicious nonsense" and "nauseating distortion."[294] It was also an example of what the Jewish Quarterly *Midstream* condemned as faulty reasoning that was transforming Eichmann "before our eyes into a symbol of the exact opposite, an innocuous man who, though now completely harmless and incapable of doing more damage, is being hounded, kidnapped and subjected to a grandstand trial and will probably be hanged in the bargain." Holocaust victims were becoming incarnate in the modern state of Israel as modern oppressors, hungry Shylocks demanding their pound of flesh; crimes against Jews "slowly transferred to the *credit* of Israel."[295] Furthermore, to judge Israel's treatment of Eichmann in a moral world which tolerated the existence of nuclear weapons was to subject it to an unduly exacting standard, to take it into an unjustified ethical realm.[296] The ethical bearing of the Holocaust witness, the survivor as expressed through Israel, was outside the conventional realm of international law, which became a "peripheral" matter of abducting another citizen in Argentina.[297]

Conservative publications recoiled at the ignorance of a prosecution case that ignored America's strategic interests. Most known among these was the *National Review*, edited by the belligerent William Buckley, Jr. Trawling through the cadaverous archive of Eichmann's crimes would, he fired in several opinion pieces, corrupt current relations between Bonn and Washington. The Cold War equation had to be considered. "The counting of corpses, and gas ovens, and kilos of gold wrenched out of dead men's teeth.... There is under way a studied attempt to cast suspicion upon Germany.... It is all there: bitterness, distrust, the refusal to forgive, the advancement of Communist aims."[298]

The sentiment was also repeated in a host of patriotic and religious publications of the Christian Right, a political force that had yet to become the dominant pro-Israel voice in American politics. Christian Zionism was still in

---

[294] John H.E. Freed, "Mayer's Nonsense," Letter, *Progressive* 25 (May 1961): 41.

[295] Schlomo Katz, "Eichmann and the Liberal 'Mentality'," *Midstream* 7, 1 (Winter, 1961): 64-7, 67.

[296] See Arthur Gilbert and Walter M. Abbott, "Christians Failed Jewish Hopes," *America* 106 (March 24, 1962): 825-8, 825.

[297] It was therefore inappropriate to expect Israel to "reach a new level of moral character": Gilbert and Abbott, "Christians," 825.

[298] "Thoughts on Eichmann," *National Review* 10 (April 22, 1961): 238-9. The theme on resurgent anti-German feeling fanned by the trial can be found in *National Review Bulletin* (April 15, 1961): 2; "Let's All Hate Germany, Comrade," *National Review* 10 (March 25, 1961): 172.

its infancy. As Novick has noted, conjuring up the anti-German ghost which could only be of benefit to the Soviets and the suspicion of "Old Testament retribution" featured as running themes.[299] The latter argument went along the lines that the vendetta waged against Eichmann was a Semitic hangover, with one Catholic paper arguing that the entire proceeding had been prompted by "vengefulness".

Taking liberties with its historical references, the Brooklyn publication *Tablet* argued that Israel was the offspring of a sinister line of Old Testamentary thought that had produced the doctrine of unconditional surrender during World War II. "Forgiveness is not in their makeup, not even forgiveness of the completely vanquished. For these warped minds there is no word as pardon."[300]

Significant in this particular column was the revaluation of Eichmann as the unjustly unpardonable, the Jews as avengers ignorant of the virtues of mercy. Periodicals such as the *Public Appeal* in Durham, North Carolina saw Israel as an outlaw while mourning for Eichmann, "dead, murdered by the international kidnappers for a crime he did not commit against a nation that did not exist."[301] Another, *Common Sense*, printed in Union, New Jersey, boasted a severe masthead "Communism is Treason," and similar views of its North Carolina counterpart.

"If he committed a crime, it was not in Israel, for Israel was not in existence then." There were no gas chambers, it charged, and the entire thrust of the Eichmann trial was the working of a Jewish, leftist cabal to invoke U.S. interest in ratifying the UN Genocide Convention, which was pernicious for paving the pathway to world government.[302]

A particularly active critic against the trial, a certain Anton A. Coreth of Larchmont in New York, busied himself by cabling Ben-Gurion in December 1961, seeing victimhood in a very different light to that of the Israeli Premier. The true victims were Germans; their persecutors were unscrupulous Allies (some of them Jews), who tried Germany after the war.

"Let us go to the bottom of the pit and bring to trial the exterminators of the German people like Churchill, Roosevelt and Truman, Morgenthau etc. etc. and all the officers who carried out their orders". As for the number of

---

[299] Novick, *Holocaust and Collective Memory*, 129.

[300] Quoted in Novick, *Holocaust and Collective Memory*, 129-30.

[301] Quoted in AJIHR, "Reverberations," 4.

[302] *Common Sense*, "Jews Commit Heinous Crimes," May 15, 1961, 1 and "The Eichmann Trial and the Genocide Convention," 2. Enclosed in envelope Christian Educational Association, Union, NJ to J. Edgar Hoover, FBI, Washington D.C., Folder 65-65842-Sec. 1, 1 of 3, Box # 25, Class 65: Espionage, RG 65, NARA, CP, MD.

Jewish victims, the figure of six million "has never been proven and cannot be proven."[303]

Even in a less cranky contribution to *Life* by Harry Golden, editor of a small publication called the *Carolina Israelite* and a staunch advocate for minority rights, feared the results of such a trial. The proceedings would yield "revelations" that would be "likely to prove embarrassing to some of her [Israel's] closest friends in the western world."[304]

In so far as "the advancement of Communist aims" was concerned, proponents were to be found on all sides. In any case, the effect was the same: a reductionist view of Eichmann's colossal crimes, a warning to guard against a greater, far more pressing historical enemy: Bolshevism. In response to Hannah Arendt's controversial reportage of the trial in the *New Yorker*, some Holocaust survivors themselves feared any interpretation of the event that would ignore the crimes committed under the hammer and sickle. One letter, written by a survivor who had immigrated to the United States from Rumania, warned that Arendt's critique of Eichmann might be construed as an overlooking of communist excesses. "To the fascist crimes against the Jews, related by you, must be added the most serious of them, that of having rehabilitated Communism to some degree, when, in fact, the crimes and iniquities of the communist regimes, in comparison with the horrors which occurred at the initiative of the Hitlerists, only seems less than they actually are." The "solidarity" that linked Stalin to Roosevelt and Churchill had to be "broken" to avoid debasing "the past history of the peoples today fallen into suffering under Soviet domination in order to justify, from an ethical, moral and political point of view, communist expansion in countries which have been independent, enjoying the benefits of the civilisation of the free world".[305]

These contradictory positions probably explained why the political slant from the State Department and White House was fairly coy on the matter of Eichmann. Washington did not send a single official observer to the trial. The

---

[303] Anton A. Coreth, National Chairman of The Monroe Doctrine National Party, Larchmont, New York, Telegram to Prime Minister Ben-Gurion, Tel Aviv, Israel, December 13, 1961, enclosed in S. J. Papich to Mr. Brennan, FBI, "Adolf Eichmann Information Concerning," February 5, 1962, Memo, in Folder Eichmann File 65-65842-Sec.1, Box #25, Class 100, RG 65, NARA, CP, MD.

[304] Harry Golden, "A Stranger to the Human Race," *Life* 50 (April 21, 1961): 43-6, 44. Amongst these was the "closed doors" argument and the reluctance on the part of the Allies to bomb the railway lines to Auschwitz, at 44.

[305] Asra Berkovitz to Hannah Arendt, Undated in Correspondence, Survivors of the Holocaust, ---A-F---1961-1966, n.d. (Series: Adolf Eichmann File, 1938-1968, n.d.), Hannah Arendt Papers, Library of Congress, Washington, D.C..

behaviour of its representatives at the Security Council was perplexing. Initially, Henry Cabot Lodge, the U.S. representative to the UN unreservedly approved Argentina's position on the case, that its sovereignty had been impugned by enterprising Mossad agents, and that due reparation be made. Lodge had not, observed the *New York Times*, even considered "what was meant by 'reparation.'"[306]

The U.S. resorted to the generalities of international law. The *Times* was content speculating that Lodge's confusion was simply a case of weighing up an assortment of variables, feeling that espionage incidents such as that of the U-2 spy plane did not mean that the U.S. repudiated sovereignty – Latin American countries such as Argentina had no reason fear.

In time, Lodge switched positions, amending the resolution to emphasise a balance between the precedent of kidnap and a need to acknowledge Eichmann's victims.

The Italian representative Egidio Ortona put it most succinctly: the Eichmann case was a matter of "reconciling ethics and law."[307] But in this process of reconciling the realms of ethics and law, the nations of the Security Council were spectators looking at an unfolding of the extraordinary paradigm of victims in judgment, or at least, the victims' judgment as conveyed through the vicarious acts of Israel.

Once he had allayed the confusion in the Department, Lodge even left room for personal reflection, juggling the politics of both the defendant and the victim in his speech to the Security Council in June 1960. The Holocaust victims come to the fore; as a witness to the corpses at Dachau, which had only recently been captured, he recalled "the memory of those literally thousands of piled-up bodies [that] will stay with me through life." The entire problem of Eichmann the abducted "could not be considered apart from the monstrous acts with which Eichmann is charged."

Any Security Council resolution could not excise the victim from its purview. "We must make it clear that not only do we not condone the monstrous acts with which Eichmann is charged; we remember them with horror and with boundless pity for his victims."[308]

---

[306] *New York Times*, "State's Confusion," June 26, 1960, E9.

[307] Quoted in *United Nations Review*, "Security Council Acts on Argentina's Complaint to Meir Against Israel," 7 (August 1960): 14-15, 15.

[308] *Department of State Bulletin*, "Security Council Considers Argentine Complaint on Eichmann Case," Statement of H. C. Lodge, June 22, 1960, 43 (July 18, 1960): 115-117, 115.

The Arendt Debate

The Arendt critique of Eichmann's trial provided a critical junction in how U.S. political and public discourse framed the Holocaust as a paradigm of victim and executioner. It provided a point of reference as to how Americans viewed the unfolding of the Holocaust within the workings of Israeli justice. In an Israeli court, the victims' entitlement to be heard (the six million voices) was considered so deafening as to drown out the reservations of the defendant and his legal team. On one level, Arendt's thesis was a counter-narrative to the unfolding of the Holocaust as an event of dignified victims fighting irredeemable evil. It even touched on the complexity that Levi articulated on the morally ambivalent positions of the victim and executioner. The aim for Arendt was the attainment of justice, one that could only come after a careful weighing up of the respective positions. For Arendt, the interrogation of the Holocaust by the Hausner prosecution provided no such weighing up, muddling ethics with law. The debate evoked by her thesis brought the politics of the Holocaust victim and defendant into stark relief.

The effect of her thesis was to undermine victim-worship that was becoming the mainstay of Holocaust public-political discourse. The trial, in shaping the Holocaust as a memory of the victim and the fundamentally evil nature of its perpetrators (the SS, the Third Reich) set up stark, moral boundaries. Such dualism, for the totalitarian thesis of Arendt's formulation, proved nonsensical, ignoring the very system that eschews such difference. As Arendt wrote in a seminar paper for discussion amongst Jewish students at the University of Chicago, Eichmann was "accused of what he did himself, not of the system within which he functioned. This system is only the background to what he did."[309]

Arendt's first salvos of criticism came in the *New Yorker* as a trial correspondent. For Arendt, Anglo-American approaches to conceptualising the nature of such atrocities as those committed under Nazi Germany were faulty. "To fall back on an unequivocal voice of conscience ... signifies a deliberate refusal to take notice of the central moral, and political phenomena of our century."[310] Eichmann, an ordinary man, had abided by the words of Hitler

---

[309] H. Arendt, Seminar Paper for Jewish students, University of Chicago, October 30, 1963, Private Reply to Jewish Critics – 1963, Box 45, Adolf Eichmann File, 1938-68, n.d., Hannah Arendt Papers. For the influence of environment on Eichmann's genocidal prowess, see Cesarini, *Eichmann*.

[310] Hannah Arendt, *Eichmann in Jerusalem: A Report on the Banality of Evil, Rev. Version* (New York: Penguin Books, 1994; orig. 1963), 148.

since his words had the force of law (*haben Gesetzeskraft*). The Nuremberg and Eichmann trials prescribed "that human beings be capable of telling right from wrong even when all they have to guide them is their own judgment, which, moreover, happens to be completely at odds with what they must regard as the unanimous opinion of all those around them."[311] The Jerusalem court merely isolated Eichmann the virus, rendering him the singular proponent of madness, a deranged killer fully cognisant of conventional evil. This was confused, according to Arendt, as it failed to distinguish norms from exceptions and rules and orders.[312] One could not violate the law in the Third Reich, which had reversed the proscription "Thou shalt not kill" since evil had lost "the quality of temptation."[313] Evil was not only banal, it was part of an apparatus that destroyed moral consciousness.

While Arendt's reporting from Jerusalem might be interpreted as a critical juncture in the development of Holocaust consciousness it also disrupted the prospects for a clean bill of ethical and moral health for the Jewish people: evidently, some Jews "had accepted the standards of the Final Solution,"[314] having either gone to their deaths quietly, or actively participated in it. Jewish organizations had been culpable; they sold out, they betrayed their flock to the Nazi authorities. It is on this point that she received greatest criticism, on this level that the Holocaust became a moral reference for Jewish martyrdom and moral supremacy, a supremacy challenged by the notion that evil is not "radical", and thus pervasive and borderless. In one of her seminar discussions, Arendt made the point clear: evil is "banal in the sense of a hair-raising superficiality", having "no roots", being "a surface phenomenon". The Eichmann trial never achieved justice because the past was never mastered; the trial instead acted as a therapeutic means for "sentimental" memory. "The extent of the catastrophe, the moral catastrophe, we can only now slowly realise. We shall have to come to terms with it, but not by sentimentality and evading the issues."[315]

The savage response by influential publicists revealed that such a moral diagnosis had no place in the emerging Holocaust consciousness of the Jewish

---

[311] Arendt, *Eichmann in Jerusalem*, 294-5.

[312] Arendt, *Eichmann in Jerusalem*, 149, 292.

[313] Arendt, *Eichmann in Jerusalem*, 150.

[314] Arendt, *Eichmann in Jerusalem*, citing the Kasztner Report (1961) 132. Rudolf Kasztner worked with a fellow leader of the Hungarian Jews, Joel Brand in brokering an agreement with Eichmann in conjunction with the War Refugee Board and the Jewish Agency to save mostly wealthy Jews, after the payment of a price (a Blut für Ware (Blood for Goods) policy). He was murdered in March 1957.

[315] Arendt, Seminar Paper for Jewish Students, 3.

victim and the absolute evil of the Holocaust executioners. Banal evil had the disturbing effect, it was said, of normalising the radical nature of Nazism. Norman Podhoretz, editor of the conservative Jewish periodical *Commentary*, wrote that Arendt's view of the Holocaust was "all cleverness and no eloquence", ridding "her story of melodrama".[316] Jewish victims had lost their "psychology" and "history"; in "place of the 'monstrous' Nazi was the 'banal' Nazi."[317] But a key error, claimed Podhoretz, was Arendt's ignorance of "the unprecedented and revolutionary character of the Nazi regime."[318] She had rationalised the Nazis in the manner that the appeasing Chamberlain had done to "Herr Hitler", assuming "that the Nazis were rational beings and that their aims must therefore be limited and subject to negotiation."[319] Podhoretz was also incredulous at the notion that Jews could have resisted. Arendt's answer: "I never and nowhere pretended that resistance had been possible. On the contrary, I praised the Warsaw Ghetto uprising because it was so to speak, 'impossible.'" As for the notion of Jewish cooperation, Hausner had created a "smokescreen" by discussing camp resistance, a "silly and cruel" question precisely because it obscured "Cooperation by Jewish leaders."[320]

Podhoretz's reaction was repeated in various Jewish and non-Jewish publications of variable repute and quality, vigorously embracing the narrative of the valiant victims, martyrs of resistance rather than meek subjects of submission. Their accusations were based on Arendt's purported lack of sympathy for Jewish "heroism," at a time when the image of the heroic Sabra Jew was dominating the mythology of the new Israel. The Jews fought, argued a trenchant piece by a New York Rabbi in the *Hillcrest Jewish Center Bulletin*, "with such tenacity, resourcefulness and skill as to even win the praise of the Nazi butchers." The Warsaw Ghetto was unparalleled in its "heroism".[321] Another Rabbi was "disturbed [at the suggestion] that there could have been Jews so lacking in decency as to collaborate with the Nazis in the extermination of their own people." Instead, it was fitting for Jews to avoid the counsel of such bodies as the American Council for Judaism in seeking to

---

[316] Norman Podhoretz, "Hannah Arendt on Eichmann: A Study in the Perversity of Brilliance," *Commentary* 35 (September 1963): 201-8, 201.

[317] Podhoretz, "Hannah Arendt on Eichmann," 205, 201.

[318] Podhoretz, "Hannah Arendt on Eichmann," 207.

[319] Podhoretz, "Hannah Arendt on Eichmann," 204.

[320] Arendt, private reply to Podhoretz, "Talk." September 18, 1963, in Folder Private Reply to Jewish Critics – 1963, Adolf Eichmann File, Hannah Arendt Papers.

[321] "Rabbi's Message," *Hillcrest Jewish Center Bulletin*, New York, record in Folder United States, Jewish, Unfavourable, 1962-1963 (Series: Adolf Eichmann File, 1938-1968, n.d.), Hannah Arendt Papers. See also *New York Times*, "Rabbis Eulogize Warsaw Heroes, 20th Anniversary of Ghetto Uprising," April 21, 1963.

chide Israel for its treatment of Eichmann, and focus on the "beneficial world-wide effects" of the trial, and the growing record of credible Jewish resistance to the Nazis.[322] One response to the *New Yorker* articles went further, claiming that Arendt was one of "the greatest enemies" amongst the Jews.[323]

TRIAL REFLECTIONS

The Eichmann trial, and reactions to it, generated a new appraisal of the Holocaust and the moral nexus between victims and executioners. The Nuremberg trials were distinguished as having been unduly general; the law of nations was condemned as antiquated and indifferent to the ethnicity and identity of human victims. There was much approval of the trial in the United States, with Israel receiving praise for finally giving voice to the victims of the Final Solution. Israel was revered, both as the bringer of justice, and the appropriate medium for Jewish retribution. There was an acceptance on the part of Gellhorn, Musmano, and such Congressmen as Hubert Humphrey and Jacob Javits that Eichmann was an example of radical evil that had to be punished. Israel was portrayed as a civilized nation, despite being exceptional, given over to disseminating justice.

This produced confusion. Law had been used, not to shape international jurisprudence as was the case at Nuremberg, but as a tool towards reaffirming an ethnic identity, a heroic redemption of victims and a total condemnation of the executioner. This did not sit comfortably with advocates such as Taylor.

The characterisation of the executioner's rights was also up for debate. Some observers, including anti-Semitic groups and various religious organs, argued that Eichmann had himself been a victim of Old Testament injustice and brutality, something of a dramatic role reversal. More complex was Arendt's unsettling examination of the defendant's attributes. The executioner was shallow in his evil, a creature of social conditioning and superficial ideology. Nor had his victims suffered solely from German executioners. Jewish groups had also participated in the scheme of elimination. Such modern evil, being shallow, could insinuate itself into situations, events. The only solid ground in countering it was international law, however flawed, since it returned the notion of punishment to an international realisation of crimes

---

322 Rabbi Jacob J. Weinstein, "The New Yorker – Eichmann and the Enemies Within": A Response to Hannah Arendt's fearsome indictment, Letter, *K.A.M News*, April 19, 1963.

323 Max Nussbaum, "Dr. Nussbaum Replies to 'New Yorker' Articles," Congressional Replies to 'New Yorker' Article 48, 16 (May 2, 1963): 1, 4.

against the human status. But for those who sought to interrogate the complexities of the victim-executioner relationship such as Arendt, criticism was forthcoming. Musmano was particularly harsh, as were Jewish figures in the United States, keen to assert Eichmann the executioner as a radical phenomenon of evil unencumbered by critical analysis. In effect, the Final Solution became a totemic human tragedy above and beyond the pragmatism of state conduct.

Chapter 4

RECONCILIATION AT BITBURG

By the 1980s, the Holocaust had been "entrenched" in American political discourses, with the Jewish victims coming to the fore as the singular sufferers of World War II. But how these debates imagined Germany within the confines of its guilty past was quite another matter. In the realm of U.S. foreign policy, the framing of the Holocaust on the politics of the victim and executioner proved malleable. It could be critically interrogated, reshaped as a tool of moral import, and employed conveniently to further policies. The politics of memory surrounding the victim and executioner fluctuated to accommodate strategic considerations. The Americans as arbiters over such politics initiated the rites of forgiveness and reconciliation of German guilt and responsibility. At Bitburg, a political reality was confirmed: that the Holocaust did not prove a bar to establishing and maintaining good relations with the Federal Republic of Germany. Forgiveness, or at least a reconsideration of the dimensions of German guilt, could become the symbolic preserve of a third party, in this case, the American president.

This form of political therapy provided very combustible material in debate. As the Holocaust became an unmistakable presence in American life, the clash between America's rehabilitation of Germany in the foreign arena and the domestic reluctance to reconcile Germany in American collective memory seemed inevitable. The representation of the Holocaust within these narratives was split between various visions which came to the fore at Bitburg. Again, as we saw in reactions to the Eichmann trial, the politics of commemorating the victim clashed with that of the executioners. Two American visions of the atrocities perpetrated against Jews came to the fore: the Wiesel version, marked by the unforgiven (the Holocaust as a disfigurement of humanity that could not be healed); and that of Reagan's political panaceas towards his anti-Communist West German ally, redemptive, somewhat amnesiac, even foolish. These visions collided on the plane of "public relations." The negative reaction to the Bitburg ceremony was, in the words of Reagan's White House Chief of Staff Donald T. Regan, "an appalling public relations disaster".[324] The wording by Regan was notable for its interpretation of Holocaust memory in lax terms – the *New Republic* was scathing of the Reagan administration's use of spectacle and theatre. "Are Reagan and his aides really so ignorant and insensitive that they see the war and the Holocaust entirely in terms of public relations?"[325]

The conflict between American visions of the Holocaust as a normative construct, untouchable in morally exceptional terms on the one hand and policy of rehabilitation of an old foe on the other was revealed in much social and intellectual comment. This tension was as much a matter of two political interpretations of the Holocaust in the United States, as it was to do with Reagan's moral confusion. As *Commonweal* editorialised, "More truly than any moment in his tenure, it has revealed the president's deep inner human disconjunctions."[326] This is not to say that the entire Reagan administration condoned the visit. A letter from Reagan's security advisor Bud McFarlane to his German equivalent the month before the visit emphasised how the Bitburg visit had succumbed to a "number of unique and almost surreal factors" that threatened "real damage to the [U.S.-German] relationship." Most major magazines and newspapers disagreed with the visit, finding fault with the political manipulation of Holocaust memory by the administration. America's Jews were most alarmed, and McFarlane noted "the truly overwhelming tide of criticism which has emerged in the American Jewish Community".[327]

A few publications even went so far as to suggest alternative ways Reagan might have given the speech before the graves. *Harper's* notably weighed into the debate. It sought to convey the moral difficulties in coping with the crimes, citing the need to balance the position of the victims with those of the perpetrators. Do not, urged the editorial, "confuse the executioners with the victims". That would presuppose an understanding of the inscrutable. "Who

---

[324] Donald T. Regan, *For the Record: From Wall Street to Washington* (San Diego: Harcourt, Brace, Jovanovich Publishers, 1988), 257.

[325] Editorial, "Symbolism and Public Relations," *New Republic* 192, 20 (May 13, 1985): 7-8, 7.

[326] Editorial, "Bitburg and the Century of Ash," *Commonweal* 112, 10 (May 17, 1985): 293-4, 293.

[327] McFarlane to Horst Teltschik, April 18, 1985, reprinted in part in G. P. Shultz, *Turmoil and Triumph: My Years as Secretary of State* (New York: Charles Scriber's Sons, 1993), 548-9, 548.

among us can unravel the awful mysteries of obedience, belief, compliance, ignorance, hatred, and cruelty that led the dead among whom we stand to the acts that horrify us?"[328] Instead, the article insisted that the Holocaust be seen as a lesson: "It is our capacity to understand that we too – perhaps even without knowing it – might become executioners."[329] Such circumspection was the reverse of Reagan's: to emphasise the ease with which one could become an executioner in the complex world of Holocaust discourse, rather than expand the prospects for victimhood, which Reagan surmised were very much possible before the threats posed by communism. For Reagan, the West could become the victims of another Holocaust, albeit one dictated from a supposedly "evil" Moscow.

The Bitburg discourse crystallised U.S. approaches to the Final Solution in the specific context of its relationship with Germany. It was a foreign policy of compromise: the clemency boards took over from the Nuremberg trials and modified the responsibility of the executioners through lessening the gravity of their crimes against humanity. Cold War necessities trumped the campaign against Nazism. The Nuremberg trials were regarded as necessary, but not morally insuperable in preventing any reconciliation between the Allies. "The American people," urged a conciliatory Byrnes to a gathering of Germans at Stuttgart in 1946, "want to help the German people win their way back to an honorable place among the free and the peace-loving peoples of the world."[330] In actual fact, German rehabilitation proved to be "miraculous", in Josef Joffe's words, "more miraculous than the rehabilitation of France after 1815."[331]

EXECUTIONERS WITH VIRTUES

By the time Reagan visited the Bitburg military cemetery, Roosevelt's desire to see Germany suffer had receded into distant memory. The sufferings of the soup kitchen had been replaced by the triumphs of the *Wirtschaftswunderland* and the pressing considerations of the NATO alliance.

[328] Pater Marin, "Words, for the President, Upon Laying A Wreath," *Harper's* 271 (July, 1985): 11-12, 11.

[329] Marin, "Words, for the President," 12.

[330] Senate Committee on Foreign Relations, *Documents on Germany*, 42; Ziemke, *U.S. Army in the Occupation of Germany*, 443.

[331] Quoted in Thomas A. Schwartz, "The 'Skeleton-Key' - European Foreign Policy, European Unity, and German Rearmament, 1949-54," *Central European History* 19, 4 (December 1986): 369-85, 369.

A penitent Chancellor Helmut Kohl sought American dispensation from guilt, hoping to forge a history for a West Germany freed of the atrocity dramas that had plagued its consciousness. He was also concerned about the commemorations in Normandy for VE-Day, to which he was uninvited. It was an occasion marked by visible differences in the Alliance.[332] Reagan notes in his memoirs that he "agreed with [Kohl] that it would be an appropriate moment for us to mark not only the fortieth anniversary of the end of World War II, but also the beginning of forty years of peace and friendship between the two nations."[333]

This dimension of U.S.-German relations puzzled the historian Arthur Schlesinger, Jr., who found it "hard to understand the sudden need for additional reconciliation in 1985."[334] *Commonweal* also found it needless, an unnecessary display of political insensitivity. "To most Americans [Kohl's desire for reconciliation] was a surprising request, one they had granted a generation ago."[335] This was the characteristic benevolence shown by American forgiveness for its ally, reformed and willing to fight the Soviet Union, the "evil empire" poised with gulag and nuclear arms behind the Iron Curtain.

American Jews and veterans were furious at the political uses of the event, unimpressed by the stock Cold War rationales. It left Elie Wiesel aggrieved. "That place [Bitburg] Mr. President, is not your place ... Your place is with the victims of the SS."[336]

The geographical metaphor of Wiesel's warning served to highlight the malleability of Holocaust imagery in the political affairs between the United States and the German Federal Republic. Within the United States, the Holocaust as framed in cultural and official discourses proved to be a totemic moral lodestone, beyond interrogation and questioning. It had become solemn in its moral intensity, the mere questioning of which constituted a violation of ethics and sensibilities. But in the territories of the perpetrators, U.S. foreign policy took a quite different turn. The space was to be viewed differently; here, the perpetrators were portrayed as victims of totalitarian evil. It was a different perception of tragedy, an Americanization of atrocity that was pitched at a different audience. One commentator went so far as to claim that

---

[332] *Time*, "The Divisive VE-Day Anniversary," 125, 20 (May 20, 1985): 32-3.
[333] Ronald Reagan, *An American Life* (New York: Pocket Books, 1990), 376.
[334] Arthur Schlesinger, Jr., "The Rush to Reconcile," *Wall Street Journal,* May 9, 1985.
[335] Editorial, "Bitburg and the Century of Ash," 294.
[336] Quoted in UPI, "Reagan Rejects Plea to Cancel Cemetery Visit," *Los Angeles Times*, April 21, 1985, Part 1, 1, col. 4.

Reagan had Americanised the event: "Mr. Reagan treated the matter as if it were an internal American affair."[337]

The atrocities were not, in this narrative, the product of a singularised evil born out of anti-Semitic exceptionalism but a more complex interlacing of political factors, namely anti-totalitarian impulses. Reagan was clouded by what he saw as a world choked by the totalitarian menace that had adopted some tendencies of Nazism: a red totalitarianism represented by such agents as the Sandinistas in Nicaragua, and the Soviets in Afghanistan. A portion of Reagan's speech on May 5 at the U.S. Air-Base at Bitburg illustrated the universalism of the argument. The cult of Holocaust victimhood was not specific, but a political universal threatened by world communism. "Today, freedom-loving people around the world must say: 'I am a Berliner, I am a Jew in a world of anti-Semitism, I am an Afghan, and I am a prisoner in the gulag'".[338] His response to the fanfare of condemnation was expressed privately: "The press … really are sucking blood and finding every person of Jewish faith they can who will denounce me."[339]

Wiesel's warning was thereby ignored, with Reagan preferring to frame the Holocaust paradigm of victims and executioners with different perspectives and strategic outlooks. At a March 21, 1985 press conference, we find Reagan arguing that the guilt complex was a needless weight on a modern Germany.

The German people, he argued, had "a guilt feeling that's been imposed on them, and I think it's unnecessary."[340] In his memoirs, Reagan reiterated how it was not "right to keep on punishing every German for the Holocaust, including the generations not yet born in the time of Hitler." Not "all Germans deserve to bear the stigma for everything he did." But Reagan significantly brought his initial experience on seeing the concentration camp inmates (an experience that was itself a deception) into line with his view of a guiltless modern Germany. The faces of those Germans who discovered "for the first time what Hitler had done" were etched on Reagan's memory. "I knew from the looks of sickening disbelief and disgust on their faces."[341]

Reagan returned a sense of dignity to the executioner, a being devoid of will, an agency crippled by the totalitarian apparatus. The German dead at

337 Geoffrey H. Hartman, *In the Longest Shadow: In the Aftermath of the Holocaust* (Bloomington, IN: Indiana University Press, 1996), 64.

338 Quoted in William L. Chaze, James Hildreth, Jeannye Thornton and Thomas J. Foley, "The Rebound Begins," *US News and World Report* 98, 19, May 20, 1985, 26-30, 29.

339 Quoted in Morris, *Dutch*, 524.

340 Quoted in *New Republic*, "Symbolism and Public Relations," 7.

341 Reagan, *An American Life*, 380.

Bitburg were "human beings crushed by a vicious ideology."[342] Like the slain in the concentration camps, there were some children amongst the executioners who went to their deaths against their will. Many of the soldiers were mere "teenagers", and Reagan implied that both the death camp and the field of battle served as turns of the same ideological system, ruining such figures of innocence as children. "There is a boy buried there who died a week before his sixteenth birthday."

That boy represented the phoenix that never rose, for, had he lived, he would "have joined his fellow countrymen in building this new democratic Federal Republic of Germany, devoted to human dignity, and the defense of freedom that we celebrate today."

The boy served as the democratic leitmotif of German integrity. His children might have been amongst the Bitburg gathering, dedicating themselves to preserving peace and "guarding the security of the free world."[343] The modern Germany, argued Reagan, had become a good agent of commemoration for the Holocaust, turning "former concentration camps into museums of death containing the most horrifying pictures you have ever seen," and encouraging German school children to pay visits to these sites.[344]

This view was further expressed by Reagan in correspondence with the World Jewish Congress representative Kalman Sultanik, letters which came to light six years after the event. Reagan was taken by one particular, bizarre theme: that of the protective SS soldier. In what proved to have little concrete historical foundation, Reagan told Sultanik, on advice from faulty German sources, that some of the SS soldiers buried at Bitburg had died protecting various inmates. "They had been executed for trying to shield inmates from torture and the ovens."[345]

In one sense, Reagan touched upon the complex ambiguities inherent in the grey zone of ethical complicity described by Primo Levy; the victim and executioner were not so ethically distinct from each other, their moral engagement close and contradictory. But Reagan never expanded on complex moral dilemmas the potential his noble SS soldier opened up to him, nor his moral limitations as an outsider to the plight of the victims. The SS soldier instead became the serviceable motif of political reconciliation. Kohl's role in

---

342 Reagan Speech, Bitburg Air Base, May 5, 1985, in *Department of State Bulletin* 85 (July 1985): 8-11, 8.

343 Reagan Speech, Bitburg Air Base, May 5, 1985,8.

344 Reagan, *An American Life*, 380.

345 Quoted in Editorial, "Reagan on Bitburg Six Years Later," *Arkansas Democrat-Gazette*, April 23, 1991.

this cleansing affair of history "lay in the hope that Ronald Reagan could in some small degree help to redo or undo German history."[346]

His Bitburg speech also introduced the feature of reconciliation in an incommensurate way: by imposing a regime of forgiveness on his Jewish audience. Survivors of the Holocaust were told to cease worrying; reconciliation did not mean "forgetting" past injustices and wrongs. "No, we will never forget, and we say to the victims of the Holocaust: Never again."[347]

This was most starkly illustrated by Reagan's reference to the episode that took place in a cottage during the Battle of the Bulge, where a mother living with her young son played the role of an impromptu arbitrator between a German soldier and his American counterpart. Both soldiers had stumbled across the particular cottage, a chance meeting that became a metaphorical setting for broader themes of reconciliation. Fearing imminent slaughter in the household, she intervened to quell any potential disagreements. The two men were asked to lay aside their weapons for a meal. A "tearful" grace was said and a "private armistice" made.[348]

At Bergen-Belsen, Reagan's somewhat opportunistic foray into the politics of Holocaust commemoration continued. *Time* was impressed, calling Reagan's display "a skilful exercise in both the art of eulogy and political damage control."[349] But here, Reagan chose to distinguish between the radical nature of Jewish suffering, and the strategic interventions around it. Understanding Jewish suffering was beyond him, in Delbo's sense, an impossible type of suffering, "useless knowledge" that could only limit the future engagement of the living. "What we've felt and are expressing with words cannot convey the suffering that they endured. That is why history will forever brand what happened as the Holocaust."[350] This did not dim his sense of optimism as "humanity refuses to accept that freedom of the spirit of man can ever be extinguished." Even in the death camps, argued Reagan, sprang hope. The new Germany was spawned from the "freedom" that ultimately came of the Third Reich's brutalities, democracy "symbolized by the fact that most of the leadership of free Germany is represented here today."[351]

This manipulation of the politics of the victim and perpetrator in Reagan's rhetoric had some sympathetic commentators. Hugh Sidey of *Time* argued that

346 Decter, "Bitburg," 25.
347 Decter, "Bitburg," 8.
348 Decter, "Bitburg," 9.
349 "Paying Homage to History," *Time* 125 (May 13, 1985): 16-19.
350 Reagan, Speech at Bergen Belsen, in *Department of State Bulletin* 85 (July 1985): 7-8, 7.
351 Reagan, Speech at Bergen Belsen, 7.

the selection of Bitburg was based on its symbolic location in U.S.-German relations, "where there are American and German forces working together on the NATO line."[352] Conservative columnist George F. Will found the wreath-laying ceremony an appropriate gesture. German soldiers were not criminals but functional automata. The "typical German soldier was a cog in an orthodox military machine." The rationale of the conscience-driven soldier defying criminal orders, so powerful at the Nuremberg trials, played no part in Will's concept of military valour. Military realities trump moral evaluations. "No army is an arena of independent judgment."[353]

Reagan's America, keen to assert its power both as the judge and then as the ethical forgiver of the executioners of the Holocaust, was proving a formidable force to critics arraigned against the visit. According to an editorial in the *Commonweal*, Reagan's conduct was emblematic of the American character. "Like Mr. Reagan, we have a deep desire to be spared, to be rid of the unpleasant present and past."[354] Bitburg "gave the impression of wishing to recall nothing of the past except common sacrifices and a shared code of military honour."[355]

In spot surveys done across the country by the *US News and World Report*, Reagan's reputation had been only slightly bruised. The Vice-Chairman of the Democrats, Roland Burris of Illinois observed how, "People tend to let bygones be bygones."[356] A Phoenix resident flattered Reagan by seeing him as a "man [who] is trying to bridge the world together." An Indiana farmer found a well-intentioned fool: "His remarks at the concentration camp made clear his intentions, and they were honourable." A *Denver Post* poll found that 84 percent of respondents had remained for the most part unchanged by the visit.[357] Reagan's staff also played on the theme of the honourable, if slightly naive peacemaker, contending "that Bitburg showed the President to be a leader who can keep his word no matter how costly it is to do so."[358] Reagan's diary note of April 19 used a stretched historical analogy: the visit to Bitburg had placed him in the position of Captain Dreyfus, unjustly accused of disloyalty and convicted by the French authorities in the nineteenth century, his "visit to the German cemetery" having been his own "Dreyfus"

---

352 Hugh Sidey, "Reflecting on Memory and Morality," *Time* 125 (May 13, 1985): 25.
353 George F. Will, "The Ghosts of World War II," *Newsweek* 105 (April 29, 1985): 78.
354 *Commonweal*, May 17, 1985.
355 Hartman, *In the Longest Shadow*, 64.
356 Quoted in Chaze et al, "The Rebound Begins," 26.
357 Chaze et al, "The Rebound Begins," 26.
358 Observations in Chaze et al, "The Rebound Begins," 26.

Case.[359] In an interview later that year, Regan could only regard the Bitburg fiasco as one of a series of "diversions" that had marked Reagan's term in office: if it was not a hostage situation in Beirut, or the need for surgery, it was historical consciousness and the Holocaust.[360]

Even the conservative columnist Midge Decter seemed to lessen the culpability of Reagan's act of folly, viewing the Holocaust through the prism of neoconservative dogma, and its critics as "liberal" apologists[361]. In Germany, Reagan had been led down the path by Kohl; in the United States, "he had been driven to trade positions with the fiercest opponents, the pious liberals." Decter's idiosyncratic reading found that Reagan had humanised murderers in the same way liberal progressives in the United States humanised serial killers who needed to be protected from civil rights abuses. Hence their "trading" of positions, making the resurrection of the perpetrator of atrocity in the political discourse of reconciliation a "liberal" mimicry. It was to "deem an armed man who is committing a murderous assault no less a victim than the unarmed innocent he murders ... the very same view of criminal behaviour that Mr. Reagan's bitterest enemies have been promulgating since time out of mind".[362] Reagan's views at Bitburg Air Base – a universal message of egalitarian victimhood – had been the product of some liberal source, "the old liberal urge to speak of suffering in the large so as to make all suffering equal".[363]

Decter's theoretical perversions in seeing Reagan as a conservative disoriented by "liberal" notions of suffering was elaborated upon in the *National Review*. The key to the "liberal" critique of Reagan's visit was the focus on Nazi crimes as the cardinal reference point of contemporary struggles, a reference point that could not be degraded by comparisons and political manipulation. Such a preoccupation had the potential to drive a wedge between current friends while ignoring the enormity of Soviet crimes. Again, always a voice of protest against any potential rupture of the U.S.-German alliance against the Soviets, the *National Review* rolled out its Cold War critics, critical of any tendency to place the ultimate executioner of the Holocaust, Hitler, above "measure or analogy."[364] The magazine ran articles around the time of the Bitburg controversy suggesting that the focus on Hitler

---

359 Reagan Diary Note, April 19, 1985, reprinted in Reagan, *An American Life*, 378.

360 "Regan on His New Team: 'I'd Give Us a B-Plus,'" *US News and World Report*, 99, 11 (September 9, 1985): 24-5, 25.

361 Midge Decter, "Bitburg: Who Forgot What," *Commentary* 80 (1985): 21-27.

362 Decter, "Bitburg," 25.

363 Decter, "Bitburg," 27.

364 Editorial, "Satanic Force v. Evil Empire," *National Review* 37 (May 31, 1985): 13.

as the paragon of evil was misplaced, if one was to consider Stalin, who "excels Hitler and his Nazi pack by far."[365] To the east of a reformed Germany, noted the *National Review* founder W. F. Buckley, Jr., stood another Teutonic half that had neglected the true lessons of the victims. The Buchenwald anniversary saw the commemoration of fallen class heroes rather than Jews in East Berlin. Even more significantly, Buckley was convinced that "genocide" was still occurring in the GDR, though he remained scant on details. He was adamant that, in "various forms, [the] Gulag continues."[366]

Globally, the contaminant of Nazism had simply re-incarnated itself: "there is Hitlerism abounding elsewhere, except that it goes by another name: Communism." Bitburg proved to be a mere sideshow, its SS soldiers redeemable, while the current impact of communism had to be recognised. "Today, you may find yourself in a cemetery harbouring dead murderers; forty years ago you found yourself allied to the Soviet Union. Each by the plausible judgement of reasonable men, was a necessary step."[367] Hitler's state "was dead". There were more pressing dangers. "At this moment, the Soviet state is enforcing its will on the Afghan people by the use of Hitlerian/Stalinist methods: torture, genocide, starvation, the use even of chemical warfare."[368]

After Bitburg, the columnist Joseph Sobran glibly told Buckley that, the debate on the Sandinistas would have changed "if Daniel Ortega and his Sandinistas were Nazis." The Holocaust was simply another social and political construction that was referable to other contexts: the victims of the Holocaust were not unique, and the relevant, more tangible victims of Buckley's present were those, as Reagan had suggested, of red totalitarianism. The progressive liberals had been angered by Reagan's repackaging of Holocaust memory to reform executioners at the expense of victims, but they remained stiff on issues of intervention against the Sandinistas, stonewalling efforts to disrupt the Ortega regime. Buckley, fantasising in a hypothetical idiom about what the world might have looked like if Hitler had found the atom bomb, suggested that the executioner's badge – the Swastika – would have been far more effective in mobilising liberal animosity had it been pinned on the Communists of Latin America. "If Daniel Ortega wore a swastika on

[365] This came in a contribution by Eugene H. Methvin, "Hitler and Stalin: Twentieth Century Superkillers," *National Review* 37 (May 31, 1985): 22-29. Methvin offers various theories for this, many off the mark. Stalin, to give one example, was not an "atavist" like the "alien" Hitler.

[366] W. F. Buckley, "Liberalism Berserk," *National Review* 37 (May 31, 1985): 54-5, 54.

[367] Editorial, "Voting on Bitburg," *National Review* 37 (May 31, 1985): 12-3, 13.

[368] Buckley, "Liberalism Berserk," 55.

his sleeve, the liberals in Congress would be calling for an American Expeditionary Force to crush him. As he stands, he is relatively safe."[369]

Not all Americans expressed horror at the dissolution of memory taking place at Bitburg. On the contrary, argued a writer to *Time* from Sandy, Utah, Reagan did not "pay homage to the SS buried at Bitburg". He had in fact "provided a platform for the victims of Nazism to remind the world of Hitler's atrocities." Rage at Reagan's conduct, far from being a negative manifestation, was a healthy note to America's moral stature, demonstrating "that we still have a conscience."[370] Martin E. Marty wrote of reinvigorating narratives surrounding victims of Nazism. "Unwittingly and ironically, Reagan, German Chancellor Helmut Kohl and their planners and public relations people ... served to keep the story fresh in its 40th year."[371] While many Veterans' organisations expressed rage at the visit, they were divided in their responses. One officer of the Veterans of Foreign Wars noted how numerous members turned in their membership cards. He regarded them as "mad folks", who had not recognised that it was essential "for the President to strengthen relations with a country committed to NATO."[372]

We see at Bitburg an elastic interpretation of the politics of victims and executioners in the framing of Holocaust discourse. Decter went so far as to regard the Reagan visit as a species of Holocaust revision, a term which had lost its references to the reality of the events it was meant to represent. Its secret terror, its complex relations between the participants, had faded. "For let us face it: the word 'Holocaust,' even for Jews, induced by now an almost dead sensation." Commissions established to commemorate its name, "a piece of sentimental grossness on television called *Holocaust*," professors and books specialising on the subject, camera-savvy Germans "bent on recording their proud deeds for posterity" all pointed to a new realisation: a Holocaust denuded of meaning.[373] Put another way, Decter had hit upon a key observation: the denuding of the Holocaust in its international context, rendered impotent by ignoring its lessons in the scrapping forum of international affairs. Its uniqueness as an event of inimitable and yet universal relevance was challenged. "It may now be applied anywhere and everywhere, to whichever kind of violence people currently find appalling." For Decter, the

---

[369] William F. Buckley, Jr., "What If ... ?" *National Review* 37 (June 14, 1985): 54-5, 55.

[370] Jerry Borrowman, "Bitburg Backlash," Letters, *Time*, June 3, 1985, 7.

[371] Martin E. Marty, "'Storycide' and the Meaning of History," *Los Angeles Times*, May 12, 1985.

[372] Quoted in *US News and World Report*, "The Rebound Begins," 98, 19 (May 12, 1985): 29.

[373] Decter, "Bitburg," 23.

tragedy in the entire action-reaction of the Bitburg spectacle – the response from Jewish leaders in the United States, and the White House in turn – diminished the moral message of the Holocaust to the level of an "ethnic" issue, an "unpleasant instance of pressure politics."[374]

The reading of Reagan's Bitburg visit by Decter was significant in how she viewed the Holocaust in the context of American life vis-à-vis Jewish identity. Jews were constantly caught between the role of being "a holy witness" and a "lobby". To treat the Holocaust with any meaning, Jews had to observe a few lessons: the historical lessons that motivated American foreign policy during the Cold War and after. Decter's suggestions came as a series of injunctions. To remain a genuine Jew, one had to abide by them, or suffer an identity crisis of forgetfulness. American Jews had to be wary of the Munich analogy "a lesson about the need to resist totalitarianism early and with strength." Jews who suggested any need on the part of democracies to "divest themselves of the power to threaten and discipline intransigent totalitarianism, especially of the Soviet variety, ha[d] forgotten the Holocaust." There was an "obligation" on the part of the Jews to be "compassionate," merely "more clear-eyed than others about the danger to democracy in our own age."[375] The Holocaust was a moral sanction to alter international relations.

In an oddly circuitous way, Decter was returning to the importance of a strong Alliance system against communism, the need to be vigilant against totalitarianism, a version of Reagan's rhetoric, endorsed and promoted by Kohl. The politics of the Jewish victim was brought to the foreground (in a manner that it was not in the 1950s) to target communism. A letter in a later *Commentary* issue from Norwalk, Connecticut picked up on the theme, seeing in the Communists the "spiritual ancestors" of Nazism. "The West German military no longer fights for Nazism: it stands as a military bulwark for freedom against ... Communism." Bitburg was merely an instance of Communist inspired propaganda, "an attempt to smear the current German military and undermine our alliance with it and the free German people it defends."[376]

Such debates were even more significant in how they foreshadowed what would become the *Historikerstreit* in West Germany, a trenchant debate between historians that sought to investigate the boundaries of a usable German past in light of present identity, while seeking to, as some American

[374] Decter, "Bitburg," 24.
[375] Decter, "Bitburg," 27.
[376] David Solan, Letter, *Commentary* 80, 6 (December 1985): 6-7, 7.

observers like Buckley were inclined to do, focus on the Bolshevik terror.[377] The singularity of the Jewish experience as victims of the Final Solution was challenged through expanding the scope of suffering during World War II to include German "victims". One of the most trenchant figures of this movement, the historian Ernst Nolte, provided an interesting parallel to the idea of Reagan's re-reading of victim identity as equivalent between Jew and SS soldier when he argued that Claude Lanzmann's *Shoah* enabled a reading that the SS camp crews "could also have been victims in their way."[378]

Jews, in other words, were not the only victims of fascism, nor had they an enduring monopoly on suffering in the debates of cultural and political identity. The German nation had moved on, engaged in a fight against Bolshevism, a fight that was of contemporary relevance in the NATO system. Such a view provoked a belligerent response from one of West Germany's foremost philosophers, Jürgen Habermas.

In his words, "the only patriotism that does not alienate us from the West is a patriotism of commitment to constitutionalism."[379] Such a commitment was only forthcoming after the exterminatory experiments of Auschwitz, which, remarked Habermas, was the only rational way of evaluating German guilt. Rather than appealing to the more collective notion of a "*deutschnational* NATO philosophy", it was far better to assimilate the legacy of Auschwitz, the spawn in reaction to it, as "the only reliable basis of our Western loyalty."[380]

Conservative Jews rallied, finding calls for strategic foresight moving. A letter in the December issue of *Commentary* attacked Reagan's critics of his Bitburg visit as "the very ones who oppose virtually every defense appropriation and foreign involvement. They are the spiritual heirs of Chamberlain, not Churchill; of the isolationists, not Roosevelt .... In short 'Never again' – which such people fervently proclaim – made real by policies

[377] An excellent text in this field is Maier, *The Unmasterable Past*. See, further, Norbert Kampe, "Normalizing the Holocaust? The Recent Historians' Debate in the Federal Republic of Germany," *Holocaust and Genocide Studies* 2 (1987): 61-90; Rudolf Augstein et al, *Historikerstreit: Die Doukumentation der Kontroverse um die Einzigartigkeit der nationalsozialistischen Judenvernichtung* (Munich: Piper, 1987); Dan Diner, "The Historians' Controversy – The Limits to the Historization of National Socialism," *Tikkun* 2 (1987): 78.

[378] Ernst Nolte, "Vergangenheit, die nicht vergehen will" [A Past that will not Pass Away], *Frankfurter Allgemeine Zeitung*, June 6, 1986; noted in Maier, *The Unmasterable Past*, 12-13.

[379] Jürgen Habermas, "Eine Art Schadensabwicklung. Die apologetischen Tendenzen in der deutschen Zeitgeschichtsschreibung" [One sort of compensation: Apologetic trends in German Historiography], *Die Zeit*, July 11, 1986, and discussed by Maier at 45.

[380] Maier, *The Unmasterable Past*, 45; Habermas, "Eine Art Schadensabwicklung."

they fervently oppose."[381] All camps were united in the rhetoric of appeasement, Chamberlain and totalitarian apologias.

Another letter writer idiosyncratically reasoned that the Federal Republic of West Germany posed no real threat to Jews anymore. The threats had instead become very real in contemporary despotic states, whose antecedents were the regimes that had committed atrocities against the Jews. Such examples could be found in "Nicaragua, Cuba and the Soviet Union, and of course, throughout the Soviet puppet regimes in Eastern Europe."[382]

But Reagan's journey to Bitburg was not so prescient or pedagogic. It proved to be a rhetorical exercise, framing the Holocaust as a disingenuous exercise in public relations in juggling the moral positions of victims and executioners. Indeed, amidst the incompetent planning of the tour itinerary by the White House, Lou Cannon of the *Washington Post* argued that Don Regan had been observing the chain of events merely as an act of public relations: "Regan decided to wait and see how it played on the networks."[383]

In this display came the visit to the air base and Bergen-Belsen concentration camp, which had been perceived in Reagan's circle of advisors to be of paramount importance. Secretary of State George Shultz was of the opinion that such a visit had to take place.[384] But Reagan had been confused. He refused initially to visit Dachau, and so the Holocaust as public relations became the Holocaust as a neglected phenomenon ignoring Dachau on the one hand yet acknowledging the soldiers of the Third Reich on the other. Suggestions came forth across the journals on how Reagan might diminish the importance of this blunder: the *Christian Science Monitor* insisted on adding a concentration camp to the itinerary to square the moral discrepancy. "If anything, to visit a concentration camp in the company of a President's West German hosts ... can be an affirmation that the future of better conduct, or repentance and forgiveness, and the healing of enmity, is already under way."[385]

Other symbolic, public relations referents came up in suggestion: the *New York Post* felt that a visit to Konrad Adenauer's grave might not be inappropriate, nor, in the opinion of *USA Today*, would a visit to Remagen, the point where American troops first crossed the Rhine during World War II.[386]

---

[381] David C. Stolinksy, Letter, *Commentary* 80, 6 (December, 1985): 2-3, 3.
[382] Frederic Wile, Letter, *Commentary* 80, 6 (December, 1985): 3.
[383] Quoted in *New Republic*, "Symbolism," 7.
[384] Shultz, *Turmoil and Triumph*, 544.
[385] Quoted in Decter, "Bitburg," 22.
[386] Noted in Decter, "Bitburg," 22.

In truth, the weightiness of the deed did not, argued critics, plague Reagan sufficiently. Indeed, in a *New Republic* editorial, such a name like Bergen-Belsen did not "weigh heavily" on Reagan's personal mind, being only "a name ... to throw to American Jews and veterans, as part of the game of special interest politics. The Holocaust, it seems, is beyond his imagination." Reagan had committed the sin of moral equivalence in saying that "that these soldiers who died defending an evil cause were victims", much as those noncombatants "scientifically murdered in the concentration camps". [387] At a public rally of 25,000 protesters at the base of the Capitol in Washington on April 20, 1985, the Reverend Jesse Jackson went further, labelling Reagan's list of policies as creations of "madness", including paying homage to "the fascists in Bitburg ... and embracing the fascists in Johannesburg".[388]

Having then framed the Holocaust as a creature of "public relations", Reagan duly extended the hand of reconciliation to the victims by inviting prominent Jewish figures to Bitburg to face their executioners. Reagan argued on the eve of his departure that reconciliation was the main aim of the venture. "It's not going to honour anyone. It's going there simply to more visibly bring to the people an awareness of the great reconciliation that has taken place."[389] Simon Wiesenthal, one of the proposed guests, refused. The legacy of the *Sunflower* prevailed; the SS men were not to be forgiven, the victims forever holding their grace from placation. "It is theoretically possible," explained Wiesenthal to the Canadian weekly *Maclean's*, "that the man who killed my parents is buried there. I am not going to allow myself to be used to cover up their blunders."[390]

A brief survey of various Jewish responses in the United States to the visit revealed the animosity generated by the visit. Arnold Fine, editor of *Jewish Press*, a Brooklyn paper with a readership of five hundred thousand, saw his office flooded by calls and letters "bitter and anguished": "If the reaction from readers and callers is any indication, the wound the President opened up may take another 40 years to heal."[391] Harry Siegman of the American Jewish Congress observed that Reagan's adventure had triggered various shades of anti-Semitic feeling in both Europe and the United States. He was busy fielding calls and letters from both "crazies" and "cultured and civilized

[387] *New Republic*, "Symbolism," 8.

[388] The *Chicago Tribune* reproduced the photograph of the rally in "Reagan's Policies 'Madness': Jackson," *The Chicago Tribune*, Midwest Edition, April 22, 1985, 2.

[389] Quoted in Michael Posner, "In the Language of Compromise," *Maclean's* 98, 25 (May 15, 1985): 22-3, 22

[390] Quoted in Posner, "Compromise," 23.

[391] Quoted in Chaze, et al, "The Rebound Begins," 29.

people, who say in gentle tones, 'I now understand why Hitler did what he did.'"[392] Amnesiac America found its own vision of the Holocaust, but in non-American territory: the land which had been responsible for instigating it. Decter struggled to believe what she had witnessed: the reductive approach of a President on such matters as "the unquestionably settled" issue of Nazism.[393]

The wide scope of Reagan's conciliatory moves also offended those American servicemen who had seen action against the Germans. Indeed, the presence of SS soldiers at Bitburg reminded U.S. veterans of the same executioners who had massacred surrendered American combatants at Malmédy. A spectrum of religious and veterans organisations also made their voices heard, with the American Veterans Committee linking the Battle of the Bulge in the Ardennes in 1944 (spearheaded by SS elite-troops) with "the Nazi plan of total domination of Europe and furtherance of its genocidal purposes against innocent peoples."[394] Harvey Cox of Harvard University's School of Divinity called Reagan's gesture of reconciliation a misguided one, emanating from his confused self-appointment as "the high priest of the United States."[395]

At Bitburg, the manipulation of the tragedy assumed tragicomic proportions. The politics of the executioner, which Reagan insisted on playing, was paired off with that of the victim. Holocaust memory seemed to somewhat degrade in the Bitburg cemetery, a case of political sleepwalking. The *Washington Post* went so far as to regard Reagan as duped, Kohl as cunning and calculating. "The Ronald Reagan who walked stiffly into the cemetery and out again with Helmut Kohl seemed almost robot-like, *led*."[396] Even a customarily obsequious Morris described Reagan in a diary note as "*der reine Tor*: unconsciously cruel in his innocence, blind to the significance of blood in the snow, too dumb to ask the Question that will give him Pity and make him Wise."[397]

This display proved to be a poignant metaphor of deception: the stones of the Waffen SS had been covered in snow when Reagan staffer Mike Deavers and his team had been scouting the area. Deavers was himself under a cloud of felony charges, and accused of making judgments impaired by alcohol.[398] Deavers also succumbed to the temptation to view the Holocaust differently, with victims less relevant than perpetrators and culprits who showed

[392] Quoted in Chaze, et al, "The Rebound Begins," 29.
[393] Midge Decter, "Bitburg: Who Forgot What," *Commentary* 80, 2 (August, 1985): 21-7, 21.
[394] Quoted in William Bole, "Bitburg: The American Scene," in Hartman, ed., *Bitburg*, 66-79, 68.
[395] Quoted in *Time*, "Paying Homage to History," 18.
[396] *Washington Post*, May 6, 1986.
[397] E. Morris, Diary, quoted in *Dutch*, 523.
[398] Regan, *For the Record*, 261.

contrition. Reagan, in the opinion of his Chief of Staff, "took the entirely laudable and typically generous view that there was no such thing as collective guilt involving the whole German nation, and that the sacrifice of the young soldiers on both sides of the conflict had carried their memory beyond politics."[399] While Regan argued that the President had used a memory that transcended politics, he was in actual fact recognising the political reality of the U.S.-West German alliance as of primary importance. He had politicized Jewish suffering in favour of political goals.[400]

Executioners as Victims

The Bitburg commemoration showed the soldier as victim. Regan recalled Kohl's towering frame at the Oval Office, "with tears in his eyes when he invited the President to Bitburg. The youthful German soldiers buried there, he said in effect, were also victims of the Nazi regime, which had sacrificed their lives for an unworthy cause." It was a "phrase" that was planted like a seed in Reagan's political memory.[401]

Secretary of State Shultz was similarly moved by the correspondence between Kohl and Reagan. The letter from Kohl on April 15, 1985 arguing the case for the American visit (which the State Department refused to release to the public) did make, in the view of the then Secretary of State, a case to commemorate the "victims of fascist terror." By not visiting Bitburg, Reagan was refusing to administer the political medicine so craved by Germany's leaders. In Shultz's account of the letter, "it would have serious psychological effect on the friendly sentiments of the German people for the United States of America and for the Reagan administration."[402] In Kohl's words, "Even then you will not be able to satisfy all those now making public protests, but I am certain that you will meet with the understanding and support of all those who are serious about peace and friendship between our two nations."[403] Kohl had pictured Bitburg as a necessary consummation between U.S.-German relations, a point that, if not reached, would result in the demise of his government. The disasters befalling such a coitus interruptus of strategic

399 Regan, *For the Record*, 258.
400 Bole, "Bitburg: The American Scene," in Hartman, ed., *Bitburg*, 72.
401 Regan, *For the Record*, 260.
402 Shultz, *Turmoil and Triumph*, 545.
403 This portion of the letter is quoted in Schultz, *Turmoil and Triumph*, 545, where the author states that certain sections were publicly released by the German government.

reconciliation arose in a conversation with U.S. Ambassador Arthur Burns. Burns was of the view that the fall of Kohl would "hurt the Federal Republic of Germany, and this ultimately would hurt the Jews, as they would be blamed for undermining a fundamentally friendly government."[404] Even Reagan argued that retreating on the issue of Bitburg would be, in effect, "walking away from a true friend. If I did that, there goes the friendship."[405]

Kohl's position was summarised in an interview with *Time*, warning of political ruin and an identity crisis in the shade of the Holocaust. "If we don't go to Bitburg; if we don't do what we jointly planned, we will deeply offend the feelings our people." These "people" were "more than minds", having "hearts and souls." But the interview was more intriguing in how it drew the connections between debates on German-U.S. relations of 1985 with early American Cold War policy towards German war crimes. Most pointed was the reference to buried SS soldiers, who, "had they survived [...] would have been amnestied under Allied regulation."[406] The focus, Kohl emphasised, should be on those Germans who had written hundreds of letters to him, urging recognition for the role of brave men under fire and under orders. "There are letters on my desk that are heartrending outcries". One of note was authored by a woman whose brother had been "forced" to take the SS uniform and perish in it.[407] Another story involved a boy who had been two years older than Kohl, hanged "because he had run away [from the SS]."[408]

Using the same figurative language of Adenauer, who had so convincingly made the case to McCloy that Germany's sovereignty was inconsistent with the very existence of war criminals on its soil, Kohl sought to position Germany's strategic worth at the centre of American foreign policy. "American freedom, not just German freedom, is now being defended in this country." A memory heavy with atrocities was problematic to reconcile with Bonn's dedicated defence of the West. How was he to justify the "personal sacrifice" of his soldiers under the cloud of the Holocaust, or indeed the prospect of a future that might see West Germany become the site of a nuclear battleground? If the United States was insisting on making West Germany a launching pad for nuclear missiles, it was implicitly asking a sacrifice that made Germans far more than "automatons" in the alliance.[409]

---

[404] Shultz, *Turmoil and Triumph*, 549.
[405] Quoted in George T. Church, "Scratches in the Teflon," *Time* 125 (May 6, 1985): 12-14, 13.
[406] "My Objective was Reconciliation," *Time* 125 (May 6, 1985): 15.
[407] "My Objective was Reconciliation," 15.
[408] "My Objective was Reconciliation," 17.
[409] "My Objective was Reconciliation," 17.

Whatever his attempts at manipulating the politics of the executioner, Reagan's reading of the Holocaust ultimately turned on the context of strategic alliances against the Soviet Union. As *Newsweek* noted in an editorial, the true significance of Reagan's visit to Europe had not been the divisions of the Bitburg visit, but the "symbolism of the [Bonn Economic] Summit: 40 years after the war, three axis leaders and four allied leaders were sitting side by side as partners and friends."[410] Thus, in the space of American geopolitics, the Holocaust was publicly framed in a manner that expeditiously dealt with German guilt through a positive evaluation of Bonn's record as a good ally in times of historical crisis.

West Germany's Ambassador to Washington Guenther van Well played on this theme to his audience at B'nai B'rith International a few days after the Bitburg visit. The world was confronted with "a new totalitarian ideology [the USSR] challenging our common Western culture and civilization rooted in Judeo-Christian values". It was necessary to "let the terrible past and the dangers of the present guide us towards recognizing our common goals and interests."[411] The executioners of the past were the modern heroes of latter-day Cold War rhetoric.

In May 1986, the then American Ambassador to Bonn Richard R. Burt described a very different Germany to the unreformed, complicit nation that the British historian A. J. P. Taylor had vowed never to visit again. The Federal Republic, the Germany of NATO and American support, could not have thrived without the antecedent qualities of democratic merit. In Burt's words, post-war Germany would not have arisen had it not been "for a long tradition of German experiences with democracy".

At a stretch, these included, somewhat abstractly, the Hanseatic League, the Constitution authored by the Frankfurt Parliament (albeit a "stillborn" effort), and the ill-fated Weimar Republic. For Burt, the Weimar Republic was not an aberration against the tide of German history, deserving "a better historical verdict than it has been given."[412]

In Burt's historical cosmetics lay a strong historical trend: the need to reshape the image of Germany over the time scale of American foreign policy, underlining virtues while eliminating flaws. In this, Burt and his predecessors were of like mind. Conant had spoken much the same way in his Godkin

---

[410] Editorial, "Bonn Economic Summit," *Newsweek* 105, 19 (May 13, 1985): 31-2.

[411] Quoted in Marjorie Hyer, "Envoy Urges German-Jewish Reconciliation," *Washington Post*, May 22, 1985, B6.

[412] These words taken from Judith Miller, "Erasing the Past: Europe's Amnesia about the Holocaust," *New York Times Magazine*, November 16, 1986, 34.

lectures, finding a renascent Germany cleansed of its infractions against civilization.

To this, the German historian Hans Mommsen was sceptical. Burt and his employers had been too eager to Americanize Germany as an ideal, thereby introducing an optimism that was unwarranted in a dangerous game of nationalist tendencies. The casualty of this process was history in general, and the Holocaust in particular. "This positive new identity that you Americans and Chancellor Kohl want so much to encourage can boomerang dangerously here if you [keep] rewriting the past, or encourage Germans to do it. Haven't you learned that you can't play around with nationalism in Germany?"[413]

OVERSTEPPING FORGIVENESS

Bitburg demonstrated a clash of worlds between the Holocaust as seen in the United States and the Holocaust as viewed by the Reagan administration in its relationship with the Federal Republic of Germany. We find in this particular unfolding of events a different course of Holocaust debate and framing, a discourse that overcame the trope of the emblematic Jewish victim and unforgiven executioner by enlarging the scope of victimhood and endorsing the notion of forgiveness. Perpetrators of extraordinary crimes committed under the rubric of war were not beyond atonement, as they had been in the major official discourse on the Eichmann trial. Nor were the Jewish victims allowed to retain a monopoly on their suffering as absolute and incomparable. For Reagan, the Communist world remained unfree and totalitarian, its victims the modern Jews of suffering. For such journals as the *National Review*, Hitler had not found an exclusive niche in the atrocities he had sanctioned – Stalin deserved closer scrutiny in what he had done, and, by implication, his victims for what they had suffered. The outcome of this was a picture of the Holocaust in American political debates freed of its unquestionable, complex silence of suffering, its inimitability something that did not prevent it from being used on the level of public symbolism.

Reagan had effectively sought to do the impossible: arrogate to himself the power of forgiveness when, as journalist Lance Morrow opined, he could not. The bond between the atrocities of the Third Reich and their victims was

[413] Mommsen quoted in Miller, "Erasing the Past," 34. For a further elaboration of Mommsen's views, see "Suche nach der 'verlorenen Geschichte'? Bemerkungen zum historischen Selbstverständnis der Bundesrepublik" [Search for a 'Lost History'? Comments on the historical self-conceptualization of the Federal Republic], *Merkur* 40 (1986): 864-874.

not vested in Reagan but between the victims and their SS executioners. Reagan only had the power to forgive his failed assassin John Hinckley.[414] Reagan's stance was typical in Washington's contradictory use of the Holocaust in U.S. foreign policy. New events required new strategies of reconciliation. What was initially begun as an attempt to punish German war crimes was overcome through American dispensation for an ally that had contributed to the West's security in its struggles against the Soviet Union.

[414] Lance Morrow, "Forgiveness to the Injured Doth Belong," *Time*, May 20, 1985, 90.

Chapter 5

REFLECTIONS

Current debates on the significance of the Holocaust have taken it from its specific European origins and globalized its relevance. In such debates, we find the victim represented as paramount in moral importance, the executioner to be evil, whether in radical or banal fashion. Within the paradigm of victim and executioner, the politics of the victim has succeeded in manifesting itself in the discourses surrounding war crime trials, truth and reconciliation committees, and reparations for victims of atrocity.[415] This has been particularly true of such initiatives as the International Criminal Court of the Former Yugoslavia and the Rwandan Criminal Tribunal. But this has not always been the case, and certainly not in American political debates on the subject of Jewish suffering during the Second World War. While the prolific literature on the Holocaust itself, and its pre-eminent placing in American life suggests that it has become a social phenomenon domestically, its placing in the context of foreign policy has proven complex and at times morally ambiguous.

The Final Solution was, first and foremost, not framed in much American political debate as a story of victims (or, at least not Jewish victims), a fact evidenced in Washington's foreign policies towards Germany. The paradox of this lies in the fact that a distant historical calamity, a non-American event, in time achieved prominence in school curricula and commemorative programs, while being ambiguously defined in Washington's alliance with Bonn and its attitudes to another ally, Israel, in its dealings with Eichmann. The legacy of the victim could be shifted in political discourses and repositioned for political

[415] See Minow, *Between Vengeance and Forgiveness*, Chapter 4.

mileage – the emblematic suffering Jew of the Final Solution could be the Afghan freedom fighter of the 1980s fighting Soviet aggression.

Conversely, the politics of the executioners could also change within the paradigm, shifting to cope with new brutalities and new instances of oppression. Nazis were disinherited of their criminal legacies as the Cold War progressed, losing them to their substitute Soviet successors. Such a view was expressed with regularity in journals of conservative opinion as Buckley's *National Review* and Podhoretz's *Commentary*. In the field of international politics, American impressions could likewise alter. The space of Israeli justice, a caged Eichmann appearing in Jerusalem after his abduction by Mossad, catalysed the debate on the politics of the victim and executioner. The executioner was empathised with, and, in more extreme quarters, became the victim, thereby turning the ineffable moral starkness of the Holocaust on its head. Even the agent of genocide can be a victim.

The story of the Holocaust as it was developed and interrogated in American political discourses in the aftermath of occupation in World War II is a story of intervention, of third party intrusions upon the asymmetrical moral and ethical relationship between victim and executioner. The intrusion proved significant because of its various distortions in attempting to punish a defeated enemy while accepting it into the fold of the anti-communist West. We find a Holocaust that is not remembered after 1945 because its focal points are on Landsberg and German war criminals, rather than victims. Americans officials had appropriated the moral and ethical high ground through jurisprudence, fashioning the legal concept of crimes against humanity. Specific victims of the Holocaust seemed hampered by the notion of what Auschwitz survivor Charlotte Delbo called "useless knowledge" – their suffering alone was of no use, their sheer magnitude unassimilable into post-war life.[416] Ironically, this was not the case with the perpetrators, who proved useful, either as chips in political bargaining or as symbols of anti-Communist valour. Communism remained the ominous threat on the horizon throughout the later part of the twentieth century. The result in the 1950s was a severe affliction of, as Ingo Müller has pointed out, "clemency fever".[417]

There seems to be some merit to the policy of framing the concept of crimes against humanity, since it defined crimes against humans *in toto*, carefully asserting these as alien to civilization. The result was a curious

[416] Charlotte Delbo, *Auschwitz and After*, trans. Rosette C. Lamont (New Haven: Yale University Press, 1995), p. 225.

[417] Ingo Müller, *Furchtbare Juristen: die unbewältigte Vergangenheit unserer Justiz* (Münich: Kindler, 1987).

distortion of the victim's status; the victim's desire for revenge was not so much placated as avoided; the focus shifted from the specific victim to an American assumption that U.S. authorities could modify the effect and guilt of German crimes through conventional legal and political channels. Forgiveness, while it was never expressly entertained, was implied, even if, in the sense Arendt argued, it could only issue from the victim with the sovereignty to punish. This was another result of the framing of crimes against Jews as "crimes against humanity" – while meritorious in its universal appeal, the term ignored the particularity of genocide, the special appeal of the victims' moral station. In the language of civilization, as the instruments of international law suggest, the civilization of the world had been shocked, and the United States, as one of its representatives, was entitled to punish.

While scholars (Derrida, Arendt) realize a distinction between forgiveness and punishment, the sovereign assertion on the part of the United States to morally rectify the deviant German with the therapy of liberal literature and facets of the "free world" was based on one cardinal assumption: that the severity of German crimes could be modified through variable sentences. The executioners were not only punished inconsistently; their degradation never took place.[418]

In contrast, the victims were left in a historical vacuum. Even more to the point, the language used by McCloy was the language of the judge who pardoned, for those who had done their time in prison had no reason to repent further. He did not speak from the perspective of the victims, which made the unfolding of justice more problematic.

The Jewish victim was treated in a considerably different manner in the 1950s. The object then was to boost the enervated Germany for the forthcoming battles for the Free world, to enable a guilty nation to be purged. The ADL demanded that German Jews stay and fight the good fight, hoping to reconcile a fractious Germany against outside threats through getting over their lot as victims. The Jews of Decter's persuasion preferred to idealise their victimhood in order to export it, and she was willing to proffer a distinct code of memory in order to generalise totalitarianism. Communism, as the heir to Nazism, provided the context of the Cold War struggle that shaped perceptions of the Holocaust into the 1980s.

---

[418] This is a note made on the role of retributive punishment in Jean Hampton, "An Expressive Theory of Retribution," in Wesley Cragg, ed., *Retributivism and its Critics* (International Association for Philosophy of Law and Social Philosophy, Nordic Conference, held at University of Toronto, June 25-27, 1990), I, 14, noted in Minow, *Between Vengeance and Forgiveness*, 121.

The debates surrounding Reagan's visit to Bitburg revealed the tense contradictions in how victims and executioners in the Holocaust could be commemorated. The reasons were strangely enough the very same ones used in diminishing the relevance of the victim in American political debates on German war crimes in the 1950s. If we find in the United States of the 1980s a political appropriation of the lessons of the Holocaust, a European tragedy that was then Americanized as a universal principle, we also find the reverse in official attitudes to its ally, where the politics of the victim and executioner are reshaped as tactical interventions. We find a President who journeyed to a place where some of the perpetrators of the Holocaust lie in order to forgive German crimes of the past. The Bitburg dead were portrayed as human instruments of a demoniacal regime, despite some being responsible for discharging the Final Solution. Reagan's intervention was also problematic even from the perspective of American soldiers who had endured atrocities at the hands of Germans.

In one way, the forgiving nature adopted by the dissimulative practices of Reagan's rhetoric should not have been entirely dismissed. Forgiveness achieves, as Arendt says, the unexpected, since it counters the expected revenge that usually follows from the transgression.[419] "Forgiving [...] is the only reaction which does not merely re-act but acts anew and unexpectedly, unconditioned by the act which provoked it and therefore freeing from its consequences both the one who forgives and the one who is forgiven."[420] But such an act can seem disingenuous. As this work has sought to show, the framing of the Holocaust legacy as a construct of victims and executioner in America's official and foreign policy discourses did not provide a commemorative framework for Holocaust victims, but a rehabilitation regime for war criminals.

The Eichmann trial was the flashpoint between forgiveness, punishment and international jurisprudence, where crimes against humanity was developed as a weapon of parochial, national identity. American critics who favoured the thread of international law as unbroken and general, regarded the capture and manner of trial a disturbing precedent against the order of international jurisprudence. The concept of crimes against humanity was revealed to be a creature of finite boundaries, its limitations exposed by the State with a purported nexus to victims it claims to speak for. In the discourse on crimes against humanity, civilization was at stake, the criminals providing a key point

---

[419] Hannah Arendt, *The Human Condition*, 2nd Edition (Chicago: University of Chicago Press, 1998), 241.

[420] Arendt, *The Human Condition*, 241.

of reference for the punishers. In the debates surrounding Eichmann and his role in the Holocaust, Israel presented the victim's integrity as a matter of importance, with Eichmann's welfare less relevant than the grand exposure of his crimes.

This provides a key similarity with the approach of the occupation authorities in Germany, where the executioners were humanised, and some of the sentences changed. If Israel was accused of trivialising the Holocaust through punishing one monstrous figure, then the same might be said of the Nuremberg logic behind stable international law: that perpetrators of radical atrocities can only ever be the subject of a conventional penal regime. When Arendt attacked the laws used against Eichmann, it was largely based on the inadequate realization on the part of the prosecution that his acts were beyond conventional legal analysis. Conversely, the fate of the victims could only be reasoned as the tragedy of totalitarianism, a morally dysfunctional world that came closer to Levi's brutalised victims and opportunistic attempts at survival than it did to the heroic narratives that were used to attack Arendt's claims.

The key difference in the Eichmann debates from American perspectives on Germany lies in the battles that took place over how such a concept as crimes against humanity or international law could be juggled with a just punishment. Cabot Lodge sought an uneasy reconciliation in his UN speeches between the images of the concentration camp and the vision of a world governed by law. The synthesis between these visions by Lodge remained incomplete. The United States preferred to follow the dictates of international law, and foresaw a threat to international peace and security if zealous groups were allowed to capture Holocaust suspects. But international law proved a fickle animal; Israel's conduct could not be divorced from the Final Solution, nor could Eichmann's role as a mass-murderer be neglected. In this, American public and official figures had difficulty with the reality of how to position the executioner in the moral structure of Holocaust debate: to punish, but at the expense of international law? Or to punish in the name of the victims, rendered silent by the cold prescriptions of international juridical reasoning?

In the American debates on Eichmann's fate, the issue of forgiveness also surfaced; the arguments from the prosecution and American supporters of Israel excised any references to forgiveness, arguing for the necessity of punishment. The opposition to this implacable stand was considerable in some activist quarters: a few American critics assumed this to be either vengeful in an Old Testament sense (in contrast to Christian forgiveness), and dangerous in the broader sense to the stability of the U.S.-German alliance. In the machinations of U.S. foreign policy, the strategic variables of framing the

Holocaust proved complex and existential. The call from some critics was that Israel must be allowed to forgive, or, alternatively, resist the temptation of trying Eichmann itself. There was a Christianisation of the juridical process. Even if Israel had survivors of the Holocaust, there was no prerogative on its part to issue punishment. Any punishment of one seemingly inadequate defendant would trivialise the Holocaust.

Some Americans wanted to internationalise the paradigm of victim and executioner, thereby re-introducing an international forum into the context of Holocaust law and ethics by means of an independent tribunal that could bypass the politics of either executioner or defendant. The international arbiter as third party, not the victim as judge, was a dominant theme in that debate. The attempt failed, but the point was made: in international politics, the spectator of genocide may seek justice, but a flawed justice, since it can never fully accord it to the parties in question.

The problems highlighted in this inquiry affect the role played by the outsider to the atrocity. Jurisprudence can only ever seek to halt the continuation of the crime through legal procedures, panaceas that do not necessarily resolve the problem of forgiveness. One issue remains insoluble and beyond the ethical context of any legal attempts from the outside to modify it; that the victim remains the supreme agent, possessing the power to grant or withhold forgiveness. That itself can never be usurped by external witnesses and institutions. Forgiveness, it might be said, is one's inalienable entitlement.

The result is that some interpretative practices approaching the Holocaust, at least when it comes to its use in politics, have tended to ignore its complex radical nature. In the political and legal sense, the U.S. approach to a defeated Germany betrayed its tactical nature, a feature of Holocaust literature that must be read in addition to notions of an Americanized Holocaust. In future it would be constructive to suggest two layers of Holocaust scholarship and political debate in American circles: the "industry" that has grown around the Holocaust as commemorated domestically (the Finkelstein critique) and the quite different angle that shows a Holocaust shaped by the strategic considerations of foreign policy.

The tragedy behind such interpretive strategies developed in response to the Holocaust in the way it is used in foreign policy remains one of difference and tactics. On the one hand, there was the severity of the survival scenes that greeted American soldiers in 1945. But the subsequent American policies of amelioration and reconciliation, while not lacking good intentions, confused the dimensions of comprehension in coping with the tragic dynamics between

Holocaust victims and their executioners. The words of Gellhorn on Dachau remain poignant on such a distinction, since its existence was a nightmare that needed to be abolished. Surely, she wrote, "this war was made to abolish Dachau, and all the other places like Dachau, and everything that Dachau stood for, and to abolish it forever."[421]

Such abolition could never happen absolutely. The war remained after all, one that had been waged in the name of Dachau's exterminating ideal as well as against it, while the punishment of its creators was made under the cloud of Cold War rivalries and ideological fears. These interpretive strategies, whether they sought to bring the victim back from the self-abnegation of the concentration camp through heroic vengefulness (the discourse around the Eichmann trial) in judging the executioner, or an attempt to focus on the specifics of the perpetrators, whether it be the assumption that they could also be victims (Bitburg and Reagan's public relations) or objects of political reconciliation, point to an ultimate paradox of ethics and Realpolitik. It certainly remains an issue in American foreign policy to this day. The problem may prove insuperable, leaving us with Levi's glum assessment of the Holocaust as a world that excludes laws, be they applicable to the living or the dead, and for that reason excludes dialectical reductions or attempts at reconciliation.

[421] Gellhorn, *The Face of War*, 178.

INDEX

A

abolition, 111
Abraham, 66
adduction, 72
administrators, 40
advancement, 73, 75
Afghanistan, 19, 87
age, 66, 94
agencies, 53
aggression, 106
American Bar Association, 66
amnesia, 14, 27, 57
ancestors, 94
anger, 47
annihilation, 47, 53
Anti-Defamation League, 52, 65
appeasement, 96
appraisals, 23
appropriations, 68
Argentina, 73, 76
arrest, 72
aspiration, 2
assault, 31, 91
assertiveness, 64
assessment, 52, 58, 67, 111
atmosphere, 45
atrocities, 3, 9, 17, 31, 32, 33, 34, 35, 36, 39, 40, 43, 44, 45, 48, 56, 57, 64, 65, 66, 77, 83, 87, 93, 96, 100, 102, 108, 109
attitudes, 3, 7, 10, 13, 28, 29, 31, 105, 108
Austria, 72
authenticity, 8
authority(s), 9, 20, 22, 36, 40, 45, 46, 53, 61, 63, 67, 68, 71, 72, 78, 90, 109
automata, 90
awareness, 97

B

bacillus, 17
Balkan atrocities, 3
ban, 8
bargaining, 7, 106
barriers, 62
base, 56, 96, 97
Belgium, 47
bending, 41
benefits, 36, 54, 75
benign, 13
blood, 87, 98
Bosnia, 4
Britain, 17, 49
brothers, 62
brutality, 14, 28, 38, 39, 80

C

capitalism, 42
case law, 42

catharsis, 7
Catholics, 47
Central Europe, 16, 29, 44, 85
challenges, 44
chaos, 37
chemical, 42, 92
Chicago, 5, 15, 30, 43, 57, 68, 69, 72, 77, 97, 108
Chief Justice, 19
Chief of Staff, 38, 84, 99
children, 63, 88
Chile, 46
China, 50
Christian Right, 73
Christian symbol, 21
Christianity, 19, 21
Christians, 20, 73
circulation, 70
citizens, 35, 53, 54, 67, 68, 70
civil rights, 91
civil service, 40
civilization, 1, 4, 22, 32, 58, 101, 102, 106, 108
clarity, 7, 18, 48
classification, 14, 58
classroom, 67
climate, 57
closure, 2
coffee, 70
cold war, 57
Cold War, 2, 6, 9, 17, 22, 23, 27, 29, 30, 31, 42, 45, 56, 58, 73, 85, 86, 91, 94, 100, 101, 106, 107, 111
communism, 7, 19, 23, 24, 29, 56, 85, 87, 92, 94
community, 9, 29, 47, 49, 52, 54, 69, 71
compensation, 9, 95
compilation, 41
complexity, 77
compliance, 85
comprehension, 110
conception, 67
conditioning, 80
conference, 87
confession, 13
confessions, 39
conflict, 2, 11, 19, 21, 52, 69, 84, 99
conformity, 41
Congress, 41, 47, 64, 65, 66, 75, 88, 93, 97
consciousness, 3, 7, 9, 10, 57, 62, 78, 86, 91
conspiracy, 42, 45
Constitution, 101
construction, 92
consulting, 1
contaminant, 92
controversial, 19, 29, 56, 60, 75
controversies, 15
cooperation, 79
cosmetics, 101
counsel, 42, 79
criminality, 20, 22, 33, 41, 44
criminals, 2, 7, 16, 22, 24, 29, 31, 37, 44, 45, 47, 49, 50, 52, 53, 54, 55, 58, 70, 90, 100, 106, 108
critical analysis, 81
criticism, 20, 37, 42, 60, 61, 77, 78, 81, 84
Croatia, 70
Cuba, 96
culture, 4, 6, 64, 101
cure, 32
currency, 38
curricula, 105

D

danger, 45, 94
death penalty, 21, 37
deaths, 12, 22, 78, 88
defects, 69
defence, 6, 24, 48, 69, 100
defendants, 45
degradation, 25, 43, 107
democracy, 48, 89, 94, 101
Democrat, 5, 88
Department of Justice, 1
depth, 9, 35
destruction, 15, 24, 55, 60
diachronic study, 11
dichotomy, 7
diet, 43

dignity, 11, 87
diplomacy, 2, 4
disaster, 84
disgust, 87
disposition, 38, 64
distortions, 106
dogs, 33
dominance, 9
drawing, 4
dualism, 15, 77
due process, 72

E

Eastern Europe, 96
editors, 57
education, 5, 34
elaboration, 22, 102
election, 50, 58
embassy, 50, 53
empathy, 28, 71
employees, 46
employers, 102
endurance, 11
enemies, 27, 62, 80, 91
energy, 27
England, 48
environment, 77
equality, 44
espionage, 1, 76
ethical mission, 2
ethics, 7, 9, 13, 21, 24, 25, 76, 77, 86, 110, 111
ethnic groups, 29, 32
ethnicity, 22, 31, 80
euphoria, 29
Europe, 7, 17, 44, 45, 48, 49, 50, 51, 63, 97, 98, 101
evidence, 5, 9, 34, 35, 39, 41, 46
evil, 1, 5, 7, 8, 10, 13, 15, 16, 20, 27, 36, 48, 61, 77, 78, 79, 80, 85, 86, 87, 92, 97, 105
evolution, 15, 62
exclusion, 42
execution, 13, 36, 37, 38, 42, 60, 64
exercise, 4, 35, 89, 96
expertise, 63
exploitation, 8
exposure, 109
extradition, 72

F

fabrication, 16
fainting, 72
faith, 68, 87
fat, 57
FBI, 5, 60, 74, 75
fear(s), 5, 55, 57, 66, 71, 76, 111
Federal Bureau of Investigation, 60
feelings, 12, 28, 100
fever, 44, 106
fights, 94
financial, 9, 36
flaws, 65, 101
flight, 34
flowers, 59
fluid, 7, 45
force, 15, 16, 25, 39, 44, 47, 56, 69, 78, 90
forced reconciliation, 2
foreign policy, vii, 2, 9, 10, 11, 15, 21, 23, 27, 36, 48, 58, 83, 85, 86, 94, 100, 101, 103, 105, 108, 109, 110, 111
formation, 38, 49, 50
framing, vii, 6, 10, 15, 21, 22, 30, 31, 32, 56, 83, 93, 96, 102, 106, 108, 109
France, 44, 49, 85
free world, 44, 64, 65, 75, 88, 107
freedom, 12, 44, 53, 65, 87, 88, 89, 94, 100, 106
friendship, 86, 99
functionalism, 4
fusion, 13, 67

G

genocide, 1, 4, 20, 58, 66, 92, 106, 107, 110
God, 28, 63
governance, 16, 40
governor, 36

gravity, 55, 85
grotesque, 34
guardian, 65
guilt, 15, 18, 25, 27, 41, 50, 54, 69, 83, 86, 87, 95, 99, 101, 107
guilty, 28, 40, 70, 83, 107

H

hair, 78
hard currency, 8
healing, 44, 96
health, 78
Henry Ford, 41
heroism, 79
history, 6, 9, 14, 18, 33, 57, 58, 61, 67, 75, 79, 86, 89, 101, 102
host, 73
hostilities, 30
House, 18, 59, 71
human, 2, 7, 14, 20, 22, 25, 34, 50, 63, 67, 69, 78, 80, 81, 84, 88, 108
humanitarian intervention, 1
humanitarianism, 23

I

ideal(s), 9, 16, 23, 30, 52, 62, 102, 111
identification, 67
identity, 8, 11, 12, 20, 22, 61, 68, 69, 80, 94, 95, 100, 102
identity politics, 68
ideology, 7, 14, 28, 80, 88, 101
idiosyncratic, 39, 91
image(s), 2, 35, 41, 56, 61, 71, 79, 101, 109
imagination, 97
immigration, 4
imprisonment, 50, 53
impulses, 87
incarceration, 31
individuals, 37, 43, 45
indoctrination, 34
industry, 8, 110
ineffectiveness, 16
infancy, 74
inmates, 12, 28, 37, 38, 42, 43, 87, 88
innocence, 15, 63, 88, 98
insane, 32
institutions, 35, 110
integration, 17, 44, 51
integrity, 88, 109
intelligence, 2
international affairs, 93
International Criminal Court, 105
international law, 20, 21, 37, 60, 62, 63, 69, 70, 71, 72, 73, 76, 80, 107, 108, 109
international relations, 94
interrogations, 39
intervention, 25, 92, 106, 108
intrusions, 58, 106
Iron Curtain, 44, 45, 46, 86
irony, 69, 70
Israel, vii, 5, 6, 8, 9, 10, 11, 13, 16, 20, 21, 23, 36, 59, 60, 61, 62, 63, 64, 65, 66, 67, 68, 69, 70, 71, 72, 73, 75, 76, 79, 80, 105, 109
issues, 9, 44, 78, 92

J

Japan, 17, 55, 61
Jewish Community, 84
Jewish immigration, 4
Jews, 3, 4, 6, 7, 15, 16, 19, 20, 22, 24, 25, 29, 31, 32, 33, 40, 47, 49, 52, 55, 56, 58, 60, 61, 62, 63, 64, 66, 67, 68, 69, 70, 73, 74, 75, 78, 79, 83, 84, 86, 92, 93, 94, 95, 96, 97, 100, 102, 107
journalists, 56, 66
juridical conflicts, 7
jurisdiction, 44, 68

K

kidnapping, 60, 70, 71, 72
kill, 78
Korea, 50
Kosovo, 4

L

landscape, 34
Latin America, 76, 92
law enforcement, 5, 68
laws, 31, 58, 60, 62, 66, 109, 111
lawyers, 68, 69
leadership, 66, 89
legality, 60
liberation, 11, 28, 29, 33, 46
liberty, 65
lice, 34
light, 5, 6, 16, 57, 58, 69, 74, 88, 94
limestone, 10
loneliness, 30
love, 28, 65, 71
loyalty, 95

M

machinery, 11
magazines, 84
magnitude, 13, 106
majority, 16, 53
man, 14, 19, 27, 33, 44, 47, 59, 65, 67, 72, 73, 77, 89, 90, 91, 97
manipulation, 4, 11, 18, 84, 89, 91, 98
manpower, 45
Maryland, 28
mass, 37, 38, 41, 47, 58, 60, 109
matter, 22, 27, 48, 49, 52, 58, 67, 73, 75, 76, 83, 84, 87, 90, 109
medicine, 99
membership, 69, 93
memory, 1, 4, 7, 9, 11, 16, 19, 27, 31, 32, 43, 50, 58, 65, 76, 77, 78, 83, 84, 85, 87, 92, 93, 98, 99, 100, 107
mental health, 71
mental processes, 37
metals, 13
metaphor, 7, 86, 98
Middle East, 71
military, 34, 36, 37, 45, 51, 54, 85, 90, 94
military courts, 37
mimicry, 91
Minneapolis, 72
miscarriage, 39
mission, 2, 5, 65
modelling, 71
Modern Age, 56
modifications, 31
monopoly, 56, 95, 102
morality, 25
Moscow, 53, 54, 85
motif, 7, 88
murder, 28, 32, 37, 40
museums, 88
mythology, 79

N

narratives, 4, 11, 83, 93, 109
nation states, 29
national identity, 108
national interests, 2
National Party, 75
national security, 56
nationalism, 18, 69, 102
NATO, 85, 90, 93, 95, 101
Nazi Germany, 1, 2, 17, 56, 60, 77
Nazi holocaust, 9
negativity, 58
neglect, 17
negotiating, 53
negotiation, 79
New England, 4, 8, 14
Nicaragua, 87, 96
nuclear weapons, 73

O

Obama, 1
obedience, 85
obstacles, 40, 50
occupied territories, 58
officials, 9, 16, 29, 42, 50, 51, 54, 106
OMB, 1
omission, 17

oppression, 5, 55, 106
optimism, 89, 102
optimists, 52
organ(s), 60, 80

P

parallel, 95
parents, 97
Parliament, 101
parole, 22, 31, 33, 49, 54, 55, 58
participants, 5, 7, 15, 21, 51, 93
password, 27
patriotism, 70, 95
peace, 44, 45, 46, 53, 66, 85, 86, 88, 99, 109
pedagogical motif, 7
penalties, 16
perpetrators, 9, 11, 18, 40, 45, 49, 50, 52, 67, 77, 84, 86, 98, 106, 108, 109, 111
personal responsibility, 66
persuasion, 107
pessimism, 58
Philadelphia, 64, 65
photographs, 35
platform, 48, 93
playing, 69, 98
poetry, 45
policy, 3, 6, 10, 15, 16, 18, 24, 32, 33, 35, 36, 37, 43, 44, 47, 48, 51, 52, 53, 57, 68, 78, 84, 100, 106
policy makers, 51, 57
political force, 73
political leaders, 9
politics, 2, 4, 6, 10, 11, 13, 15, 17, 19, 21, 23, 25, 28, 29, 44, 45, 47, 48, 52, 55, 58, 60, 64, 67, 73, 76, 77, 83, 89, 93, 94, 97, 98, 99, 101, 105, 106, 108, 110
population, 45
portraits, 12
pragmatism, 41, 52, 81
precedent(s), 15, 37, 42, 66, 69, 70, 76, 108
preservation, 12
president, 2, 19, 23, 36, 39, 42, 49, 52, 53, 67, 83, 84, 85, 86, 90, 93, 96, 97, 99, 108
President Obama, 2
prevention, 4
principles, 16, 20, 23, 41, 54, 58, 66
prisoners, 12, 28, 34, 37, 39, 44, 47, 53, 58
prisoners of war, 34, 37, 47, 58
prisons, 22, 44, 50
prognosis, 49
propaganda, 34, 94
proposition, 51
Protestants, 47
psychology, 4, 71, 79
public administration, 15
public figures, 61
public opinion, 29, 30, 46
publishing, 15
punishment, 13, 21, 22, 30, 31, 33, 34, 37, 40, 41, 48, 54, 60, 61, 63, 64, 65, 80, 107, 108, 109, 111

Q

qualifications, 6
questioning, 86

R

race, 28, 32
ratification, 50
reactions, 10, 33, 34, 64, 71, 80, 83
readership, 67, 97
reading, 11, 13, 19, 35, 56, 91, 94, 95, 101
reality, 7, 9, 11, 24, 57, 72, 83, 93, 99, 109
reasoning, 41, 69, 73, 109
recall, 90
recognition, 23, 100
recommendations, 53
reconciliation, 2, 19, 23, 51, 71, 83, 85, 86, 88, 89, 91, 97, 98, 100, 103, 105, 109, 110, 111
recovery, 15
reform, 40, 92
refugees, 3
rehabilitation, 16, 17, 52, 83, 84, 85, 108
relatives, 39, 47

relevance, 8, 10, 19, 31, 36, 65, 93, 95, 105, 108
relief, 13, 77
religion, vii, 3, 22
repackaging, 16, 92
reparation, 76
repellent, 33
reputation, 90
requirements, 60
resentment, 45
resistance, 55, 79
resolution, 49, 76
resources, 17
response, 18, 39, 42, 64, 73, 75, 78, 80, 87, 94, 95, 110
restitution, 52
restoration, 10
retaliation, 14
retribution, 32, 74, 80
revaluation, 74
rhetoric, 10, 16, 17, 18, 21, 22, 36, 56, 58, 61, 69, 89, 94, 96, 101, 108
righting, 72
rights, 1, 16, 38, 48, 63, 64, 69, 70, 75, 80
risk, 14, 52
Roman Catholics, 6
roots, 78
rule of law, 69
rules, 31, 60, 66, 69, 78
Russia, 30
Rwanda, 4

S

sadism, 28
safety, 40, 67
schema, 12
scholarship, 13, 14, 15, 110
school, 88, 105
science, 17
scope, 15, 41, 42, 95, 98, 102
Second World, 28, 31, 105
security, 7, 30, 32, 49, 51, 84, 88, 103, 109
self-concept, 102
Senate, 40, 41, 51, 54, 85
sensation, 93
September 11, 5, 6
Serbs, 70
serial killers, 91
shade, 100
sham, 23
shame, 34
shape, 80
shock, 29, 35, 36, 57
shoot, 28, 38
short supply, 38
skeleton, 44
slavery, 43
social life, 9
socialism, 24
society, 1, 36, 65, 66
solidarity, 18, 75
solution, 17, 29, 49, 63
sovereignty, 22, 23, 30, 54, 62, 68, 76, 100, 107
Soviet Union, 56, 86, 92, 96, 101, 103
specialists, 49
species, 66, 93
specter, 56
speculation, 33
speech, 65, 66, 76, 84, 87, 89
Spring, 31, 56, 57, 61, 64
SS, 11, 12, 24, 27, 28, 33, 34, 38, 39, 54, 77, 86, 88, 92, 93, 95, 97, 98, 100, 103
St. Petersburg, 9
stability, 17, 30, 109
starvation, 92
state(s), 4, 11, 16, 29, 30, 36, 43, 47, 54, 60, 61, 62, 64, 67, 69, 73, 81, 92, 96, 99
statehood, 62
stigma, 87
stock, 86
stomach, 35
stress, 22, 54
structure, 4, 109
suicide, 35
Supreme Court, 37, 64, 66
survival, 4, 12, 28, 109, 110
survivors, 5, 11, 31, 36, 38, 58, 63, 75, 110
symbolism, 101, 102

sympathy, 52, 60, 64, 79
synthesis, 109

T

tactics, 2, 4, 38, 110
target, 37, 94
techniques, 5
teeth, 73
tension(s), 7, 84
tenure, 84
territory, 69, 98
terrorist activities, 1
terrorist attack, 6
theatre, 24, 36, 60, 84
theoretical reduction, 6
therapy, 24, 25, 83, 107
Third Reich, 4, 11, 16, 17, 36, 53, 55, 56, 57, 77, 78, 89, 96, 102
threats, 2, 39, 56, 85, 96, 107
tobacco, 39
tones, 98
torture, 88, 92
training, 38
transgression, 108
trauma, 23, 70
Treasury, 29
treatment, 2, 13, 22, 29, 47, 61, 69, 73, 80
trial, 6, 7, 8, 11, 13, 15, 16, 19, 20, 21, 30, 31, 36, 38, 40, 41, 50, 60, 61, 62, 63, 64, 65, 66, 67, 69, 70, 71, 72, 73, 74, 75, 77, 78, 80, 83, 102, 108, 111

U

U.S. policy, 52
UN, 58, 63, 74, 76, 109
unconditioned, 108
uniform, 2, 54, 100
United Nations, 76
universality, 71
USA, 96
USSR, 101

V

vacuum, 14, 107
variables, 30, 76, 109
venue, 63
violence, 28, 93
viruses, 49
vision(s), 18, 44, 83, 84, 98, 109

W

waiver, 1
walking, 12, 59, 100
war, 2, 4, 6, 7, 10, 15, 16, 18, 19, 22, 24, 28, 29, 30, 31, 32, 34, 36, 37, 38, 42, 44, 45, 46, 47, 48, 49, 50, 52, 53, 54, 55, 56, 58, 61, 70, 73, 74, 84, 100, 101, 102, 103, 105, 106, 108, 111
war crimes, 2, 6, 15, 17, 19, 28, 29, 30, 31, 32, 36, 37, 38, 42, 48, 50, 52, 61, 73, 100, 103, 108
Washington, 6, 10, 11, 17, 23, 29, 36, 41, 44, 49, 50, 55, 56, 60, 63, 64, 68, 73, 74, 75, 84, 96, 97, 98, 101, 103, 105
weapons, 89
welfare, 2, 11, 22, 23, 30, 31, 37, 40, 43, 44, 47, 54, 58, 68, 109
well-being, 46
Western Europe, 45, 51
White House, 50, 75, 84, 94, 96
withdrawal, 64
witnesses, 63, 65, 110
workers, 43
World Bank, 43
World War I, 3, 17, 19, 25, 39, 56, 62, 74, 83, 86, 90, 95, 96, 106

Y

Yale University, 3, 61, 106
yield, 75
Yugoslavia, 105